D1150186

What do I do now?

What do I do now?

Getting going on the Christian life

Paul Harris
& Nick Pollard

edited by
Martin Cooper

Inter-Varsity Press

INTER-VARSITY PRESS
38 De Montfort Street, Leicester LE1 7GP, England
Email: ivp@uccf.org.uk
Website: www.ivpbooks.com

First published 2004

British Library Cataloguing in Publication Data
A catalogue record for this book is available from the British Library.

ISBN 1–84474–062–5

Set in Monotype Dante 10.5/13pt
Typeset in Great Britain by CRB Associates, Reepham, Norfolk
Printed and bound in Great Britain by Creative Print and Design (Wales),
Ebbw Vale

Inter-Varsity Press is the publishing division of the Universities and
Colleges Christian Fellowship (formerly the Inter-Varsity Fellowship), a
student movement linking Christian Unions in universities and colleges
throughout Great Britain, and a member movement of the International
Fellowship of Evangelical Students. For more information about local and
national activities write to UCCF, 38 De Montfort Street, Leicester
LE1 7GP, email us at email@uccf.org.uk or visit the UCCF website at
www.uccf.org.uk.

Contents

Editor's foreword

Martin Cooper

If there is one thing that my thirty years of work with growing Christians have taught me, it is that getting to know Jesus has little to do with how people come to faith, but very much to do with what happens to them after that momentous step.

Just as young children need a loving, caring environment, with a good diet and plenty of opportunity for education and exercise, so young believers in Christ are significantly helped, after their initial commitment to him, by having the right kind of follow-up.

That is what this book is all about. It will help new Christians to begin the Christian life focusing on the things that are most important in laying a foundation for knowing and following Jesus – 'the elementary truths of God's word'.

So, how did it come into being? First, I worked out a structure and wrote many pages of notes on the topics that are essential for every Christian to grasp: the Bible; God; prayer; the church; sin; lifestyle; relationships. Then Nick Pollard and Paul Harris (who are both also very experienced in helping new Christians) turned these into text for the book, drawing illustrations from their own lives and experiences, and added a few extra chapters by way of introduction and ending.

Both Inter-Varsity Press and I then edited the whole text,

suggesting amendments and additions to make the book easy and clear to understand.

So, whatever their journey to faith, it is our hope and prayer that this book will enable new Christians to start confidently on a lifetime's journey of living as a Christian, but will also provide a framework of basic truth around which to do further reading and study.

Martin Cooper
The Navigators
www.navigators.co.uk
May 2004

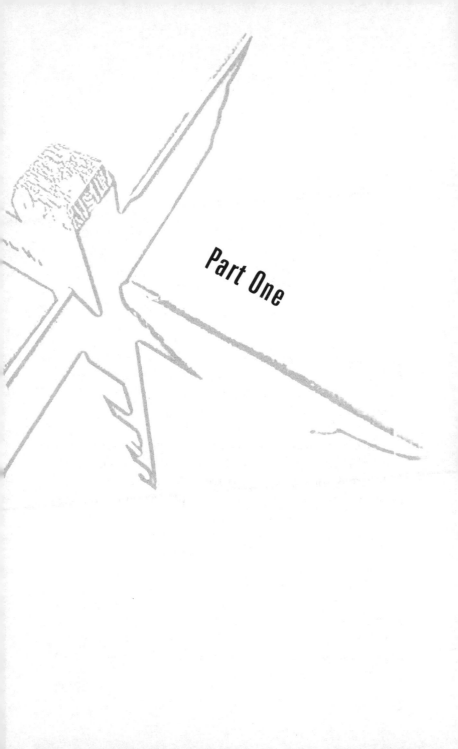

Part One

1

Welcome

Nick Pollard

Congratulations! If you have just become a Christian, then I think you have made the best decision of your life. In fact, in many ways you have started out on a whole new life, in a new relationship with God. Jesus described it as like being born all over again.

I have been with many different people when they have become Christians. I have often had the privilege of helping them as they took their first step, praying to commit their lives to Christ. And in almost every case, after praying, they have asked the question 'What do I do now?'

That's a great question. Here you are, with your new life, and you want to know what to do with it. What do you do now? It is quite like when a baby is born.

I have had two babies. Well, I didn't actually have them myself – my wife did that because she was better equipped than me. But I was there when they were born. It's an awesome experience to see this new life emerge. I remember, with my first child, picking him up, holding him, kissing him – and then thinking to myself, 'Now, what do I do with this, then?'

Perhaps I expected some kind of an instruction book to arrive with him – because everything else you get comes with a little book. Get a new television – there's a little booklet; get a DVD player – there's a set of instructions; get a new car – there's an owner's manual. But when a baby has been born – you can wait as long as you like, there's no little booklet!

My wife and I tried to figure things out on our own. We discovered that a baby is essentially a digestive system with a loud noise at one end – and no responsibility at the other. One of the things I learned was that babies love to be jiggled. My son, in particular, used to love it when I lay on my back, held him up in the air directly above my face – and jiggled him. I learned that this would make him smile. One day, through a rather messy experience, I also learned not to do it just after he had been fed! I remember thinking, as I wiped myself clean, 'If only this new life had come with an instruction manual!'

Looking back on that now, I realize how similar it was to the thoughts I had just after I became a Christian. I committed myself to following Jesus at 10 pm on Sunday, 25 June 1972, when I was fifteen years old. I remember the mixture of excitement and uncertainty that I felt as I walked home that night. I was excited that I had, at last, come into a real and proper relationship with God, who made me. I was excited about what would happen next, and what it would mean to walk and talk with God day by day from then onwards. But I was also uncertain what I should do to develop this relationship. I did not even know whether it would last, or whether it would just fizzle out.

When I got home and sat in my room, I picked up my Bible and it dawned on me – I was holding in my hands the instruction manual I would need. The Bible claims to be the 'word of God'. (See 2 Timothy 3:16.) That is, it contains the information that God wants to give us, and – even more than that – God himself will speak to us through it.

So, that night, I began not just a new relationship with God, but also a commitment to read the Bible thoroughly and regularly

– so that God could always reveal to me the answer to the question 'What do I do now?' It can do the same for you.

I hope that this book will help you as you get started.

God bless you,

Nick Pollard
The Damaris Trust
www.damaris.org

2

Can I be sure I am a Christian?

Paul Harris

Belonging!

So you have become a Christian! Congratulations and welcome! Whether you realized it at the time or not, the step you have taken is massive. You may have been overwhelmed by the enormity of your decision. On the other hand, it may have been the natural, logical step after a time of cool and careful searching. We have different emotional wiring and our reaction at the time of commitment or conversion – that is, when you said 'Yes' to Jesus – may be different. But the result is the same. Whatever you did or did not feel at the time, the fact is, you now belong to Jesus. This has massive implications for the way you look at the world – your world-view. It will affect the way you understand yourself and others and influence the choices you make.

Most of us have questions before and after deciding to become followers of Jesus. I remember the student worker who helped me discover faith asking me whether I had any questions. I had many, but the one I asked then and there was 'Now I am a Christian, can I still snog girls?' Hardly a deep theological question, but a pressing one nevertheless! Nick, Martin and I frequently find ourselves in different settings, such as radio and television studios, schools, universities, pubs and parties, chatting with people who have numerous questions about Christian faith. Most of the people we meet have no experience of church – being an ex-police officer, I might say they have no previous convictions! So we have set out to deal with some of the questions that people like you and them are likely to have. This is clearly not the final word on these issues, but we hope you find what follows helpful, as you take your first steps as a follower of Jesus.

So, before we go any further, let's pick up a very common and natural question that many new Christians ask themselves. Throughout this book we will be constantly reminding you that being a Christian is about having a relationship with Jesus. Of course, there are important beliefs which form the foundation of your relationship, but we will unashamedly draw parallels with starting a relationship with a boy or girl friend. When you first start going out with someone, it can take a while for it to sink in that you really are in this relationship. How serious is it? Can you trust the other person? Will they still like you when they really get to know you? All these and other questions apply to your relationship with Jesus.

Perhaps what attracted you to Jesus initially was his offer of forgiveness. Christian faith is sometimes described as the best fresh start in life. Perhaps you were searching for a purpose in life – a challenge greater than just living to please yourself. For some people, his offer of eternal life – that is, a quality of life that begins now and which cannot be ended by physical death – is what draws them to him.

Whatever it was that drew you to him, it may come as a slight shock to be told that you now belong to him. You thought it was a freedom thing! These days, the idea of being possessed by anyone seems very inappropriate and frankly unattractive. Relax ... belonging to Jesus is different! But how?

God wants you to feel secure in your relationship with him. You may not be aware of it, but God has been making the first move in your relationship for longer than you realize. Some words from the Bible (chapter 31, verse 3 of the book of Jeremiah) express it well: 'I have loved you with an everlasting love; I have drawn you with loving-kindness.'

Some people have the idea that God will love them only so long as they manage to live some sort of good life. It is as though Christian faith is a sort of performance-related pay scheme. This leads to great effort, loads of guilt and a repetitive cycle of failure, fresh start and more failure. You were not made to be a hamster in a wheel! You do not have to earn God's love. You *cannot* earn God's love. The life he offers is officially described as a free gift. And there's no catch attached to this gift. Nothing you can do can make him love you less. Nothing you can do can make him love you more. He has your best interests at heart and in time will prove himself more faithful than even your closest relative or friend.

As with any new relationship, you may feel a range of emotions. Excitement and exhilaration, apprehension and fear are just some of the prime suspects. Feelings such as these should not be denied – they are important and a part of being human. Feelings, however, can be notoriously fickle – affected by such mundane factors as diet, sleep, hormones, or even last night's curry!

Your relationship with Jesus has much more secure foundations. It is rooted in various facts that are unaffected by shifting emotions. It is reinforced by promises that have stood the test of time and have been tested by countless of Jesus' followers before you. The most important facts are those concerning Jesus. We will deal with questions to do with Jesus later in the book. For the moment, it is important just to stress that Jesus really lived here on earth, died on a cross and came back to life. These were historical events.

The other set of facts concerns what you have done. You have probably picked up this book or been given it because you have told yourself and/or someone else that you have decided to become a Christian. You may have prayed a prayer asking for forgiveness and asking God to come into your life. Or perhaps becoming a Christian has been a long and gradual process, and now you know this is what you want to do. At this stage you probably cannot explain what happened, but somehow you sense that things are different.

There are many promises in the Bible, some of which we will look at as we go on. At this point, let's look at some words of advice given in the early days of Christianity to people who were spiritual seekers. 'If you confess with your mouth, "Jesus is Lord," and believe in your heart that God raised him from the dead, you will be saved.' (You can read these words in a book of the Bible called Romans, chapter 10, verse 9.) Notice how there is no 'maybe' about this – the words are 'you will be saved'!

In other words, if you have said to God that you believe in Jesus; that you want to know him in your life; that you are sorry for the wrong things in your life; and that you want to make a fresh start, then God takes you at your word. It's a done deal, and for his part he promises that he will never leave you and will be with you for ever – both sides of that experience we call death.

If, as you read this, you realize that you have not actually said these things to God, then you might like to turn to the last chapter of this book – 'What do I do first?' – and start there.

A final word by way of introduction. Do not worry if you have doubts over aspects of your faith. That is normal, not something to be ashamed of, and quite often the prelude to a new and deeper discovery in your relationship with God. We hope that what we have written addresses some of the doubts you may have.

So 'What do you do now?' Turn to the rest of the book. You do not have to read it in sequence, and we won't be looking over your shoulder urging you to read our particular piece! Look at the questions in the contents – and dive in.

3

Keeping going

Nick Pollard

I heard about a Christian student who was asked whether he had a favourite verse in the Bible. 'Yes,' he replied. 'It's in the book of Isaiah, chapter 5, verse 11. And it says "Woe unto them who rise up early in the morning."' What a great verse for students! The problem is, of course, that he has taken that sentence out of context. Someone once pointed out that if you take the word 'text' out of the word 'context' you are left with the word 'con'. And that was what this student was doing – conning himself into thinking that the Bible told him to lie in bed all day.

Whatever else you learn from reading this book, I hope that you will discover that God will speak to you through the Bible – but that you must read each bit of the Bible in its context. When you read a sentence or phrase, see how it fits into what the whole verse says. When you read a verse, see how it fits into what the whole chapter says. When you read a chapter, see how it fits into what the whole book says. When you read a book, see how it fits into what the whole Bible says. If you do this, you won't make the same mistake as that student. And you will find that God will challenge you and teach you how to live in his world, his way, as a follower of Jesus.

But how can you learn to read the Bible in this way? It will take time, and this book can help you get started. So let's begin now, by looking at a couple of verses from the book of Colossians:

> So then, just as you received Christ Jesus as Lord, continue to live your lives in him, rooted and built up in him, strengthened in the faith as you were taught, and overflowing with thankfulness (Colossians 2:6–7).

These verses come after chapter 1, which talks about giving thanks for the wonderful life God gives to us through Jesus. And they are followed by the rest of chapter 2, which talks about the danger of living a life that is bound up by religious rules and regulations. This message is very important for new Christians. Indeed, the whole of Colossians is a great book for new Christians to read through. Since it was originally written as a letter from Paul to the young Christians at Colosse, it has a lot to say to new Christians today. Many of the issues are the same. Why don't you sit down and read it in one go, right the way through, as you would read a letter? It will give you the proper context for looking at these two verses from chapter 2.

'Just as you received Christ Jesus as Lord, continue to live your lives in him,' this part of the Bible says. So, what are you to do now? How are you to live as a Christian? The answer is that you 'continue' ... 'just as' you started. And how was that? How did you 'receive Christ Jesus as Lord'? The answer is that you received Christ by faith, by trusting in him. You didn't have to achieve anything to become a Christian. You didn't have to pass any test or attain any particular standard. You didn't have to follow any set of rules or regulations. Therefore, says the Bible, just as you started – so continue.

Andy seemed a really keen Christian. He prayed at certain times every day; he read a certain amount of the Bible every day;

he gave a certain amount of his money to the church; he made sure that he went to every meeting that his church put on. And so the list could go on – with a catalogue of things which were great for any Christian to do. But the problem for Andy was why he did them. The fact was that Andy did these things because he thought that he had to do them in order to be a proper Christian – and that if he didn't follow his self-imposed regime, then he would fall away and lose his faith.

This was an understandable fear because, when he was very young, he had prayed some kind of prayer of commitment to Jesus – but he didn't really mean it, and his faith did not last very long. After a time of rebellion against God, when he deliberately didn't live the way that he knew God wanted him to, he later made a real and genuine commitment to following Jesus, and was now very keen not to fall away or rebel again. So he looked for any rule or regulation that he could find and tried to obey it. He looked for any religious practice he could follow – and tried to do it faithfully.

It took me a long time to help him to see that God wanted him not to be bound up with so many rules and regulations, but rather to continue to live as a Christian in the same way that he had become a Christian – by faith in Christ. That is, he should live through a relationship, not a set of rules.

Let me tell you about an illustration that helped Andy to understand this. Many years ago I asked my wife, Carol, to marry me. She said 'Yes', and for the past twenty-seven years our relationship has grown and developed. Imagine that, instead, she had said to me: 'Yes, okay, Nick, I will marry you – but here are the rules you must follow in order to be married to me.' Imagine that she set out three clear rules. First, I must give her flowers every week. Second, I must tell her that I love her every day. Third, I must give her a kiss every hour, on the hour.

Those are all great things to do – but it wouldn't be much of a relationship if it were based on being bound by a set of rules like that. Would it please Carol if she knew that, when I tell her I love her, it doesn't come from the heart but from her rule book? Would slavish obedience to these regulations develop my love for her? Of course not; in fact, these rules and regulations would damage the relationship rather than help it.

The fact is, Carol didn't give me a set of rules, but did ask me to love her. And I do love her. And because I love her I want to do loving things. So I buy her flowers – I even grow them myself in the garden. I tell her I love her – I write it on the condensation in the windows; I mark it out on the sand at the beach; I put love notes on her pillow when I go away. I do everything I can to let her know how much I love her. And I kiss her – as much as I can, as often as I can. But she knows, and I know, that I do those things because I love her, not because I am religiously following a set of rules and regulations.

God wanted Andy to do the things he was doing. He wanted him to spend time in prayer; to read the Bible; to give freely; to be a part of the church – all these things. But God wanted Andy to do them because Andy loved him, not because he was following a set of rules and regulations. And it was only as Andy realized this that he began to relax and enjoy his relationship with God. He began to understand and experience how much God loved him and wanted him to enjoy their life together, rather than being bound up with rules and regulations. He began to see that God wanted him to 'continue' by faith and through a relationship which was 'just as' he had received Christ Jesus as Lord – as those verses from Colossians chapter 2 told him.

Then those verses go on to say more. They describe a Christian life which is 'rooted and built up in him, strengthened in the faith as you were taught, and overflowing with thankfulness'. Let's unpack this a little.

First, we are 'rooted and built up in him': that is, we belong to Jesus. Let me give you an illustration.

Two years ago I planted some new shrubs in my garden. In the months that followed I tended and cared for them, until I was sure that their roots really were growing out into the soil – that is, they were fully rooted. Since then they have grown and built up new branches and leaves. So now, as I look up from my computer and out of the window, there is no doubt that those shrubs belong in the garden; they live there. They are not just visiting; this is where they belong. In the same way, when we become a Christian, we are rooted in Christ – we belong to him.

Second, we are 'strengthened in the faith as you were taught': that is, we believe in Jesus. Let me tell you a story.

When I was in America some years ago, I visited Niagara Falls. There I read the story of a man who called himself The Great Blondin. He was a tightrope walker who put a rope across the falls and walked along it. Apparently, he was very good at it and used to draw a big crowd to watch him perform various stunts, such as pushing a wheelbarrow in front of him over the falls. One day, so the story goes, he asked the crowd if they believed that he could walk across carrying someone in his wheelbarrow. 'Yes!' they shouted. 'Of course you can – you are The Great Blondin!' So he said to the crowd: 'All right: one of you get in the wheelbarrow.' As if by magic, the crowd disappeared. They said that they believed him, but they weren't prepared to trust their lives into his hands. They didn't really have faith in him.

Being a Christian is a bit like getting into Jesus' wheelbarrow and letting him push us along the tightrope of life. Christian belief is not just some list of belief statements that we have to tick off. It means learning about Jesus and then being strengthened through the faith we have in him – as we trust ourselves into his hands day by day.

Third, we are 'overflowing with thankfulness': that is, we behave in a way that expresses our love and appreciation of Jesus.

Let me at this point apologize if the church has given you the impression that this is where you should start – by changing your behaviour. My wife and I used to run an open youth club at our church. It had about 300 teenagers, who came and went at different times. We were delighted when we managed to enable some of them to feel that they belonged in the church – and to come along to other events and activities. But others in the church couldn't cope with them, because they didn't behave in the way that these others thought they ought to. So there was no way they were going to let these teenagers feel that they belonged – until they learned to behave. This, unfortunately, was completely the wrong way around.

The fact is that, throughout the Bible, we see that God calls people first of all to believe and to belong and then to behave. Some time, you might like to read through all four gospels (the books in the Bible that tell the story of Jesus' life: Matthew, Mark, Luke and John) and see this progression take place in the lives of the disciples. First of all, Jesus calls them to follow him – to live their lives with him, to belong with him. Then he teaches them – and they gradually come to believe in his claims about himself. Lastly, they begin to behave in a way that expresses their love for him. But, even at the end, they don't do this very well – on the night when Jesus is arrested and taken off to be crucified they first fall asleep, then run away or deny knowing him.

In the same way, if you have become a Christian, you now belong to Jesus; as you study the Bible, you will develop your understanding of what this means, and gradually your behaviour will change. Increasingly you will find that you behave in a way that expresses your thankfulness to Jesus for who he is and what he has done for you.

This behaviour change takes time. You might find that you get frustrated because you are not behaving in the way that you should. And you may find that older Christians get frustrated with you for the same reason.

But growth takes time. And new life is messy. Newborn Christians are rather similar to newborn babies. When we brought our babies home they created a lot of mess. One of the biggest mysteries to a new Dad like me was 'How can something so small and sweet produce so much of something so absolutely disgusting?' But our babies belonged to us. This was their home – and they believed in us, they trusted us. Then, gradually, they began to behave in a way that expressed their love and thankfulness to us.

It will be just the same for you, as a newborn Christian in the family of God.

Part Two

4

Prayer

Nick Pollard

Why pray?

If you want your relationship with God to grow and develop, you will need to spend time with him – rather like any other relationship. We spend time with a good friend, or a marriage partner, or a boy- or girl-friend, because we love them – and want to love them more. Sometimes we talk specifically about particular issues or problems; at others, we just chat about the things we're doing at that moment; often we just sit in comfortable silence; but, through it all, we are always seeking to listen and to respond. As you look through the Bible you will discover that prayer is similar to this.

The Bible shows us that sometimes we should take specific time out to talk to God about particular issues. Jesus did this a lot – particularly early in the morning, which is a really good time to pray like this. 'Very early in the morning, while it was still dark, Jesus got up, left the house and went off to a solitary place, where he prayed' (Mark 1:35). You will find that your relationship with God will grow best if you follow Jesus' example. Some Christians refer to a specific time of prayer alone with God each day as a 'Quiet Time'.

But the Bible also talks about praying throughout our everyday lives. For example, it says 'pray continually' (1 Thessalonians 5:17). That is, we should be aware of God's presence and be talking to him throughout every day. If you had a really good friend who was with you all through the day, wherever you went, you wouldn't ignore her; you would chat to her about things as they happened. It's the same with God. I spend a lot of my day on the phone, so I try to stop and pray for the person I am about to call before I dial their number. Even a prayer lasting no more than five or ten seconds keeps me close to God, aware of his presence with me and his love for everyone I speak to.

But, however we pray, prayer (as we will see later) is as much us submitting ourselves to God as it is us presenting our requests to him. Our relationships with our friends would not grow if we talked all the time and didn't listen to them – how much more so with God! Remember that God does not need us to tell him what to do – but we do need him to tell us. Prayer is not 'me trying to change God's mind so he agrees with me'; rather it is part of the process of 'me letting God change my mind so I agree with him'. That is why prayer is best accompanied by Bible study, so that we talk to God through our prayers, and he talks to us through the Bible.

Can the Bible help me to pray?

The Bible provides both a guide and an inspiration for our prayers. That is, the Bible guides us in how best to pray – and also provides us with the material to help us do it.

When the disciples asked Jesus to teach them how to pray, he told them a prayer that has become known as 'The Lord's Prayer' (see Matthew 6:9–13 and Luke 11:2–4):

Our Father in heaven,
hallowed be your name.
Your kingdom come,
your will be done
on earth as it is in heaven.
Give us today our daily bread.
And forgive us our debts,
as we also have forgiven our debtors.
And lead us not into temptation,
but deliver us from the evil one.

This is a great prayer to pray as it is. But it is also a great structure for a longer period of prayer. There are basically five parts to this prayer.

Our Father in heaven,
hallowed be your name.

We praise God for who he is – a holy and awesome God, who is like a good father to us.

Your kingdom come,
your will be done
on earth as it is in heaven.

We submit ourselves to God as our king and look forward to the time when everyone recognizes him as king and obeys his will.

Give us today our daily bread.

We recognize that we are dependent on God for all our needs.

And forgive us our debts,
as we also have forgiven our debtors.

We confess our sins and forgive others who have sinned against us.

> And lead us not into temptation,
>> but deliver us from the evil one.

We ask God to lead us and protect us.

Having a structure like that is something like having a list you can work through to keep yourself on track. If we then take that structure as a basis, we find that the Bible is full of material that will help us as we pray through each part. As an example, here are five psalms that you could use to help you pray through the structure Jesus gave:

- Praising God – Psalm 103
- Submitting to him as king – Psalm 99
- Recognizing our dependence on God – Psalm 118
- Confessing our sins – Psalm 51
- Asking God to lead and protect us – Psalm 71.

If we keep the Bible open in front of us as we pray, and use it as our guide and inspiration, then not only will we speak to God – we will also hear him speak to us through his word.

Is there a proper time and place to pray?

The Bible does not give us specific rules and regulations that we must follow about the time and place for prayer. There does not seem to be one 'proper' occasion or location to pray – any more than there is one proper time or place to kiss your husband or hug your children. We show our love to our loved ones at different times and in different places, but we always make sure we do it. And so it is with prayer.

I love being with my children. When we are on holiday, we

spend every moment of the day talking and playing with one another; but when I am working, my life is very busy and they could get squeezed out. So I choose to set aside special time to be with them each day. It's the same with prayer. Sometimes I seem to be praying all the time: walking with God; talking with him. But, when I am busy, God too can get squeezed out – so I ensure that I set aside a special time to pray each day. I don't have to do that. There isn't a rule that says I must pray a certain amount at certain times every day. But, sometimes, having a fixed time for prayer helps me to ensure that God does not get squeezed out.

My children and I love talking together – wherever we are. Sometimes we sit alone and talk for hours; sometimes it is just a quick chat in the car; sometimes we talk with others there too; and so the list could go on. My prayer life is rather similar. Sometimes I pray alone; sometimes I pray with others. Sometimes I might set aside a whole hour to pray; at other times, it is a quick prayer in the car.

How can I avoid being distracted when I pray?

You can't! You will always be distracted when you pray. It's the same in any relationship – when we talk with our friends we are often distracted; other thoughts come into our minds, or things around us catch our attention. But there are ways of minimizing those distractions – by having a structure for your prayers. And there are ways of turning the distractions into prayers.

We can minimize the distractions by ensuring that we are in a place which is not likely to distract us. If we want to have an important conversation with someone, we may close ourselves away in a room with them to ensure there won't be interruptions. In the same way, if we want to spend time praying about something specific, we can get away from those things which distract us. Go into a room on your own with God, close your eyes and focus your mind specifically upon him.

However, we don't always want to fight against distractions – because distractions can also be a good stimulus for prayer. Again this is similar to any conversation: it can wander all over the place, as we are 'distracted' into talking about anything that comes into our minds, or catches our attention.

Spending time with God is rather like that. You might be praying about one thing, when you find that you are 'distracted' by a thought about something else. Don't feel discouraged and give up praying. Instead, turn that thought into a prayer – start praying for that. Then you might be 'distracted' once more by a third thought. Again, don't feel discouraged. Turn that thought into a prayer, too. God wants us to share our lives with him. That includes relaxed conversations that wander all over the place – and not turning all of our prayers into the spiritual equivalent of business meetings.

What do I do when I don't feel like praying?

I have times when I don't feel like praying. If I didn't pray for a whole day, probably nothing disastrous would happen – life would go on. So I could easily find myself not praying for another day, and another – in fact, I could drift away from God altogether.

What can stop this from happening? The Bible tells us clearly: we are not meant to develop our relationship with God on our own, but together with other Christians. When we came into a relationship with God, we also came into a relationship with other Christians, in which prayer is important. As Jesus himself once said: 'if two of you on earth agree about anything you ask for, it will be done for you by my Father in heaven. For where two or three come together in my name, there am I with them' (Matthew 18:19).

So it is very important that you find other people with whom you can meet and pray. Perhaps a friend, or a group of friends, or a regular prayer meeting – somewhere where you will be missed if you start drifting away. Then, on the days when you don't feel like praying – you can't drift away for long. If you are surrounded by

Christians who pray with and for you, that is a good place to be. I highly recommend it.

Is prayer a waste of time?

Yes, in some ways prayer is a waste of time. When we are under a lot of pressure, with deadlines pressing in on every side, it seems crazy to stop and pray. Wouldn't more be achieved if you spent that time writing, or reading, or calling people on the phone? Perhaps it would. But then, wasting time with someone is one of the ways in which we demonstrate our love for them – and build our relationship with them.

You deliberately waste your time with someone only if you love them. Life can always feel too busy. At any time, we have work to do, calls to make, people to keep up with – the 'to-do' list is always scary. But often, if a friend gives us a call, we just waste time together. We don't achieve anything; we haven't made anything; we can't cross anything off the 'to-do' list. But it is because we love them that we want to waste time with them; that is what we do with people we love.

So, when God says to me, 'Come on – let's play!' then – if I love him – I will want to waste time with him, by walking with him; and talking with him; and sometimes just kicking the leaves together.

Will God answer my prayers?

The Bible tells us to 'present your requests before God' (Philippians 4:6). It also tells us that he will answer those prayers that are asked in Jesus' name. Jesus himself said: 'Very truly I tell you, my Father will give you whatever you ask in my name' (John 16:23).

It is important that we don't muddle up those two things. We cannot just ask for anything, add on 'in Jesus' name' at the end and expect God to grant it.

What does 'asking in Jesus' name' mean? It's like the little boy whose Mum sends him to the shops to buy things for her. If he asks for goods in his mother's name, he is able to charge them to her account. He is given them, because he is asking for what she wants and is following her instructions. It is rather like that when we are 'praying in Jesus' name'. We are asking for what Jesus wants – that is, we are identifying ourselves with his will.

How do we do this? We start by reading the Bible and asking God to show us what he wants. Then, in our prayers, we identify with his desire for us. For example, you might have read through Galatians 5:22–23, in which we are told the way in which God wants to bear fruit in our lives through his Spirit. If we then pray that God will give us more love, more joy, more peace, more patience and so on – we can end by saying 'in Jesus' name', because we are asking for what we know God wants. And we can be sure that he will answer those prayers.

But we can also present our requests before God. We can ask him for the things that we want, provided that we do so humbly and gently, recognizing that God knows what we need far better than we do. We can request of him that he would provide 'the desires of [our] heart' (Psalm 37:4). But that does not mean that God will automatically answer those prayers, because we may be asking for something which is not the best for us. In fact, as I look back on my life, I really thank God that he didn't answer all my prayers – because often I asked for things that were not the best for me, and God knew better what I needed.

However, the more time we spend in prayer, the more we will find that our minds are changed to be like God's mind – which means that, more and more, we will find that the things we want are the things that God wants. So, increasingly, when 'we present our requests before God', we will actually be 'praying in Jesus' name'. The more we do so, the more God will answer our prayers – because we will be asking him for the very things that he wants to give us.

5

Church

Paul Harris

What is church?

Church often does not get a good press! I remember a comedy programme some years ago doing a spoof advertising campaign for the church. Slogans included 'Church – it's where the table-tennis is!' and 'Church – it's better than putting your head in a deep fat fryer!' The latter showed a man with his head swathed in bandages! Headlines about declining numbers, local scandals, or bitter national debates may have left you feeling understandably wary of church. So what is the truth?

As you read on, remember that the essential thing about being a Christian is that you have a real relationship with Jesus. You are first and foremost a follower of him. You should expect to become part of a local church, but being a churchgoer or church member is always a secondary thing – important though it is!

Church is about people first and buildings second. Relation-ships first! The word 'church' can be used to describe various things. In a global, and even timeless, sense it describes all Christians everywhere, whenever they have lived. The moment you trust Jesus and begin the relationship with him, you count as part of the universal church. Labels and denominations, such as whether you are Baptist, Church of England or Methodist, do not matter. You are a Christian – one of his! That is what matters.

'Church' can also describe a denomination, like those mentioned above. They each have something distinctive about their history or the way they organize themselves. These days, many of them are prepared to focus on the central beliefs they have in common with other Christian denominations, rather than on their differences. Be wary of any group that tries to promote itself by running down other Christians!

Most of us experience 'church' locally. A church is a group of Christians who meet together in some way and share their lives together to a greater or lesser extent. They may or may not have a building of their own that they call 'church'. Some churches meet in rented premises such as schools; others meet in private homes.

Churches organize themselves in different ways. Some are more formal than others. The vast majority have some sort of Sunday meeting. For many Christians, the most important part of their church experience is about meeting with other believers to encourage and support one another in growing in their faith and in relating that faith to everyday life; this may happen in mid-week.

Church is changing. There are new expressions of church emerging. Christians are experimenting with meeting in new places: in pubs, in cafés and even on the internet! The amount of choice you have will depend on where you live.

Do I have to go to church every Sunday?

The short answer to that is ... no. People who say, 'You don't have to go to church to be a Christian!' are right. It is not going to church that makes you a Christian. That's about having a relationship with Jesus through believing and trusting in him, asking him to be central in your life and responding to the love he shows you. However, it's a funny sort of Christian who never goes to church!

Christian faith is not meant to be a private, solitary affair. It is about relationship and community. Being in relationship with other Christians helps you to grow and mature in your faith. Trying to go it alone is a cop-out and unwise. Some of us are more private than others. That's fine – there are styles of church to suit most types of person. By all means be more private, but do not try to be a secret Christian.

Changing working patterns and the demands of family and other relationships can make going to church every Sunday hard. Do not get hung up or legalistic about this, but recognize that the way we spend our time reflects our priorities. It's normally possible to find a balance. When I was younger I was a police officer for a while and had to work Sunday shifts. I was also a keen sportsman. So I had competing demands, but I found it was possible to meet with Christians at some point on a Sunday in most weeks – even if it was not always in the same place or at the same time!

This is not really a new tension. One of the earliest Christian writers advised his readers: 'Let us not give up meeting together, as some are in the habit of doing, but let us encourage one another'. (You can read this in Hebrews 10:25, NIV. For these initials, see chapter 10 on 'The Bible'.)

How do I choose a church?

There is an old saying, 'If you find the perfect church, don't join it or you'll spoil it!' The church is made up of people – none of whom are perfect – so have realistic expectations. All sorts of factors will affect your choice. In these early months and years of following Jesus it will be wise to find a church that will encourage you and help you to grow. Look out for signs that the people are passionate about Jesus and are still keen to grow themselves. Positive signs are that they take the Bible seriously and teach it; that they pray; and that they seem to be an outward-looking group of people.

Wherever you go, it will probably seem strange at first, but after a few weeks you will probably have a good idea of whether you will be welcomed and can be honest about your questions and needs.

It may well be that, before deciding to become a Christian, you have explored Christianity through a link with a local church. If a friend who is a Christian has been instrumental in your search for faith, it is probably a good idea to try linking up with their church to begin with. The style of worship varies from church to church. Some are more modern or informal, whereas others are more traditional. When people are asked in surveys why they joined a particular church, they do mention such things as the style of music, the quality of the preaching and even the coffee served afterwards! All these things have an influence, but – time and again – what comes out as most important is the quality of the relationships with other church members.

Churches are usually made up of people of different ages and from different backgrounds, although occasionally they may be slightly more 'monochrome'. One of the exciting things about becoming a Christian is the discovery that you really have joined a large new family. I have found myself in different places all over the world and been welcomed and offered hospitality and practical help by fellow Christians whom I would not naturally have been drawn to if I had worked on appearances alone. It is probably a good idea, however, to look for a church where there is at least a small group of people at a similar stage of life to your own.

When you are looking for a house, estate agents say 'Location, location, location!' That's not quite so important when church hunting, but it does play a part. It may be tempting to travel some distance to get what you particularly fancy in a church. Remember, though, that on a dark, wet night a long journey may well be a disincentive to meeting with your fellow Christians. A growing number of churches are taking more seriously the challenge to serve their local community. God's people should always be on the look-out for ways to demonstrate his love in practical ways: for example, by providing help to poor, or housebound, or sick, or elderly people; or by getting involved in local campaigns in support of vulnerable people. It is hard to feel part of this if you do not live in the area, so bear this in mind when choosing.

These days, it is not uncommon for Christians to be involved in one local church as their priority, but to visit another church in the area from time to time to make up for any deficiency in their 'spiritual diet'. This is easier when local churches are working closely together.

I suggest it may be helpful for you to read one of the first descriptions of a church. You can find it in Acts 2:42–47. It describes openness and sharing; you should look out for at least some degree of these in seeking the right church for you.

What about Baptism and Holy Communion?

These are terms that you may soon hear when you link up with a church. They describe things that Jesus commanded his followers to do and which are important in the life of the Christian. Different groups of Christians attach different degrees of significance to them; sadly, they have sometimes allowed their strongly held views on the subjects to spoil relationships with their fellow Christians. As you start out on your journey of following Jesus, make sure that you keep him at the centre of your thinking and living. As the saying goes, 'The main thing is to keep the main thing the main thing!'

Baptism is the welcome sign and initiation ceremony for a new Christian. Jesus commanded his followers to spread the good news about how people could be saved and get to know God. He said: 'Go and make disciples of all nations, baptizing them in the name of the Father and of the Son and of the Holy Spirit, and teaching them to obey everything I have commanded you' (Matthew 28:19–20).

The hearers of the first Christian sermon knew that the powerful message about Jesus they had heard demanded a response. They asked the disciples what they should do. Peter told them: 'Repent and be baptized, every one of you, in the name of Jesus Christ for the forgiveness of your sins. And you will receive the gift of the Holy Spirit' (Acts 2:38).

Christianity grew out of Judaism. Baptism and Holy Communion reflect these Jewish roots. Every Jewish baby boy was circumcised as a sign of belonging to God's people. Baptism is the sign of belonging for Christians. It is the external sign of the inner change that God makes in the life of every Christian. In baptism water is used to show the cleansing and new birth involved in becoming a follower of Jesus. Water cannot do that – only God's power can do it! Some Christians choose to baptize their children as babies, in anticipation of the day when they will decide for themselves to follow Jesus in their own right. Others prefer to dedicate their children to God, so that they can be baptized when they are older and have chosen to be Christians for themselves.

Do not feel that you are second rate or odd if you have not been baptized already. These days, the majority of people have not been! Instead, be glad that you can be baptized as a powerful and meaningful sign of the change that God has made in your life through Jesus. Talk to one of the leaders of the church you join; I am sure they will be happy to explain more about baptism and to arrange for you to be baptized.

Again, do not feel as though you're missing out if you have been baptized already, perhaps as a young child. You can be glad that God took the initiative of loving you long before you were able to love him back. You may also like to find out more about your baptism, so that it can become more meaningful for you.

As a Jew Jesus celebrated various religious festivals. One of the most important was called Passover. For centuries his ancestors had remembered a time when God had rescued them from slavery and spared them from death. Set in the context of a full meal, the Passover supper was full of symbolic meaning. Jesus wanted his followers and the church they would found after his death to have their own version of the Passover. This is what is known as The Lord's Supper, Holy Communion or Eucharist – a Greek word that means 'thanksgiving'. At the heart of the ceremony Christians take some bread and wine to help them remember that Jesus' body was broken and his blood was spilled so that we can all be forgiven. The service may be elaborate or simple, but the message is the same. Supremely it helps us to remember what Jesus did by dying on the cross. It also is an expression of belonging to a community of believers and looks ahead to the hope of heaven that we have.

You can read about the way in which Jesus started communion in various places in the New Testament, such as Luke 22:7–22 and 1 Corinthians 11:23–25.

How do I make the most of church?

It is hard to answer this question without resorting to clichés like 'It's all about give and take' and 'You get out of something what you put into it.' Try to see your involvement in a local church as something that will demand something of you at the same time as it helps you to grow in your faith. Invest time in relationships with other church members, but make sure that you don't get cut off from your wider circle of friends and family. Being part of a church is important. It should equip you to live a fruitful, attractive and intriguing life among people who as yet do not know God in the way you are getting to know him.

Try to become part of a small group of fellow church members with whom you can be yourself and with whom you can pray and study the Bible. In time, they will help you to discover how to use the gifts and abilities God has given you. Offer to take on a role of some sort in the church, but always remember that the most important work of the church usually happens outside the walls and beyond the programmes!

6

Lifestyle

Nick Pollard

Will my lifestyle change now I am a Christian?

When you became a Christian you repented – that is, you 'changed your mind'; you decided in your mind that from now on you wanted to follow Jesus, to be a disciple of his (that is, a follower and a learner). Gradually, you will discover that this will lead to changes in your lifestyle.

All relationships mean change. Imagine that two people decide to get married, but one of them says, 'But I don't want anything to change. I want to carry on going out with other people. And I want to carry on living on my own.' That would not be a very good marriage. The fact is that marriages mean changes.

In the same way, a relationship with God means changes. There are changes in the way in which we use our time and money; the places we go to; the things we do.

But, again, as in all relationships, these changes are based upon love and not on rules – as we saw back in chapter 2. If you love God you will want to do the things that please him and the things that show others how great he is. The Bible puts it this way: 'This is to my Father's glory, that you bear much fruit, showing yourselves to be my disciples' (John 15:8). God will gradually change your lifestyle so that you 'bear much fruit'. This means that as you become more like Jesus you will make a positive impact in the world. You might even influence others to think about following Jesus themselves. And you will show your 'Father's glory' – in other words, God's wonderfulness will be revealed by your life and your actions, and he will be honoured by what you are and do.

Can't I just be a Christian without my lifestyle changing?

I meet many Christians who are trying to follow Christ and to live an ungodly life at the same time. They tell me that they pray and they are part of a church – but they think nothing of getting drunk, or being sexually promiscuous, or hoarding money for themselves. The problem for them is that this double life tears them apart. God wants us to live with consistency and integrity; it is the only way to live at peace with yourself and with God.

Let me give you an illustration. Imagine you get invited out for a drink. You accept and your friend says 'Great – I've got a motorbike outside, I'll give you a lift.' Immediately after this, someone else comes up to you and invites you for a drink. Imagine that you accept that invitation also, and *he* says, 'Great – I've got a motorbike outside, I'll give you a lift.' You then go out into the car park and there they are, both of the people you said you would go out with, sitting on their motorbikes, which are side by side. Imagine that you put your right leg over one motorbike and your left leg over the other – and they head off in opposite directions. Now you're going to feel a little bit frustrated; in fact, it brings tears to my eyes to imagine what it would be like.

The point is that you cannot go in two directions at once – it will tear you apart. It's just the same with the Christian life: you cannot go God's way and the world's way at the same time. People who try to do this find themselves being torn apart.

Becoming a Christian is rather like getting off the world's motorbike onto God's motorbike, for a ride that is difficult; a ride that takes you in the opposite direction from all those around you; a ride where you feel that you are swimming against the tide; but a ride that is brilliant – and that lasts for ever.

Do I have to change my lifestyle myself?

No. You need to be willing for your lifestyle to change, but it is God who will do the changing.

The Bible says that 'it is God who works in you to will and to act to fulfill his good purpose' (Philippians 2:13). This means that it is God who is working in you, enabling you to change – he enables you to 'will' and to 'act'. That is, he changes your will so that what you want is what he wants – then you will do it.

Following Jesus will not actually be a struggle if you fully surrender yourself to God and allow him to work inside you, to change you gradually to become more and more like him. Then all you will need to do is what you want to do – because God will have changed you, so that what you want is what he wants. Then you will 'will' and 'do' his good pleasure.

How do I make decisions now I am a Christian?

As you continually surrender yourself to God and allow him to change you to be more like him you will find that, in every decision you face, you will be asking yourself 'What does God want me to do?' You will be seeking his guidance and his direction. How do you do that?

One way is to ask yourself 'What would Jesus do in this situation?' That isn't always going to give you a clear answer, because Jesus was actually God on earth – we can't always do what he did! A good friend of mine was organizing a party for teenagers, where they were each asked to bring some food. One girl came with a large pack of her favourite crisps – and was reluctant to put them down on the table. My friend asked her if she had brought them to share; she said she wanted just to eat them herself. He asked her, 'What would Jesus do if he had brought them?' Quick as a flash, she replied 'If it was him, he would just make them into enough for everybody.'

Although she really knew what the right thing was in that situation, the fact is that guidance – in other words, knowing what God wants us to do – is not always easy. If you look at great men and women of God in the past, you will find that they too have struggled with making decisions. If you read the biographies of great Christians in the past (and I highly recommend it), you will discover that they did not always find it easy to hear what God was saying to them. David Livingstone tried to go to China, but eventually God sent him to Africa instead; William Carey planned to go to Polynesia but God sent him to India; Adoniram Judson went to India, but was then led on to Burma; Dr Barnardo planned to go to China to work with Hudson Taylor, but God kept him in London to serve the poor – and so the list could go on.

Indeed, if you look in the book of Acts (Acts 16:6–10) you will see that Paul, too, struggled at first to find God's direction for the next stage of his life. Verses 6 to 8 see him travelling some 400 miles trying to find where God wanted him to be. So not knowing God's will was not an excuse for inactivity – although he did not know God's particular will for him (where he should go specifically), he did know God's general will (that he should be telling people about Jesus). In the same way, you may find it difficult sometimes to know God's particular will for you in a specific situation – but you do know God's general will for you (this book is all about God's general will for new Christians), so you can at least get on with that!

Verses 9 and 10, however, show Paul receiving some very clear guidance from God. Notice two lessons we can learn from this. First, Paul saw a vision of a man saying 'Come!' rather than a vision of God saying 'Go!' Many Christians will tell you that this has been their experience of guidance as well – that God has opened their eyes to a need which they hadn't really seen before, and which God is clearly calling them to meet. Second, Paul's response to the need that he saw was rational and not irrational. Verse 10 implies that he talked about it with his companions and 'concluded' that God had called them. That conclusion was clearly the result of thinking and talking together.

We are called to live by faith – but faith is not irrational. When the Bible contrasts this faith with an opposite, it talks about 'sight', not 'reason'. The Bible says we are to 'live by faith not by sight' (2 Corinthians 5:7); it doesn't say we are to 'live by faith not by reason'. That is, faith is reasonable; it involves using our brains. Responding to God's guidance is rational; it involves talking with other Christians. But faith means stepping out into that which we cannot yet see – and trusting God to sustain us.

What about money?

The Bible calls us to come into a relationship with God. It then warns us against those things that will stand in the way of that relationship. There are many such warnings in the Bible, but perhaps the strongest of these is the warning against the love of money. Indeed, when Jesus took one thing to contrast with serving God he took money. He said, 'You cannot faithfully serve both God and Money' (Matthew 6:24; Luke 16:13). Notice that he didn't say you cannot serve both God and sexual promiscuity; or drugs; or excessive alcohol; or many of the other things that we know can damage us and our relationship with God. He warned us against the love of money.

This warning is echoed through the rest of the Bible. Paul's first letter to Timothy (1 Timothy 6:10) says that 'the love of money is a root of all kinds of evil' and tells us that 'some people, eager for money, have wandered from the faith'.

Why is money so dangerous? Well, what does money represent? It represents a symbol for resources that we will obtain in the future. So the accumulation of money means the accumulation of future resources. This is damaging both to us and to others. It is damaging to us if we place our faith in the money we have (and which will provide for us in the future), rather than placing our faith in God (who will provide for us in the future). Thus we can find ourselves loving our money instead of God. It is damaging to other people because our accumulation of resources for ourselves in the future cuts down the availability of resources for other people today.

Does God care about my work?

Your new life as a Christian is not just a spare-time activity. God is not interested only in what you do on Sundays, but on Mondays too – and all the time you are at work. But, now you are a Christian, you have a new boss: your heavenly Father. That is why the Bible says 'Whatever you do, work at it with all your heart, as working for the Lord, not for human masters' (Colossians 3:23).

Christians ought to be the best workers, because we are seeking to honour God in all that we do – including our work. We do not see work just as some means to an end, some way of making money to fund our spare time. Work is a place where we can use the gifts and talents God has given us for the good of all. God has created us to work. When God told Adam to work in the garden of Eden (Genesis 2:15) he was showing that this was part of his plan for our lives. Work was not a problem that came after sin entered into the world; it was part of God's intention for us. But he also created us to spend time with him, and with others, and to rest and play. So God created us to have a balance in our lives.

One of the things that sin does is to muck up that balance, so that people don't want to work – or, on the other hand, can't stop working.

As you allow God to change you into the person he created you to be, you will find that he puts your whole life into balance: you will be neither a workaholic nor someone who hates work. You will find that God gives you a good balance between work, rest, play and prayer.

7

Relationships

Paul Harris

What difference does being a Christian make to my relationships?

Your new-found relationship with Jesus will affect the way you value and conduct all your relationships. It should affect your deepest friendships; your relationships with any colleagues; and the most ordinary of relationships with people like the postman or the person who sits opposite you on the bus!

Becoming a Christian forces you to see other people in a whole new light. Discovering that God made you for a purpose and that he loves you, has forgiven you and lives in you is also to discover that this can be true for every other human being who crosses your path.

Experiencing God's forgiveness should mean that I will be more understanding and forgiving of others' weaknesses. I wish that were automatically the case. Jesus was clear that the willingness to forgive others was one of the hallmarks of the genuine follower. Having given his disciples the prayer outline known as The Lord's Prayer, which includes the line 'Forgive us our debts as we forgive our debtors' (Matthew 6:12), he rammed home his message by saying: 'For if you forgive others when they sin against you, your heavenly Father will also forgive you. But if you do not forgive others their sins, your Father will not forgive your sins' (Matthew 6:14–15).

Cathy, my wife, and I use some written prayers each morning to help us start the day. Having listened to the news and gulped our first swigs of tea, we read a few Bible verses. Each morning has different prayers, with space for us to add our own. We know that each day will bring challenging encounters. On Wednesday mornings we pray these words:

> Show to me this day amidst life's dark streaks of wrong and suffering the light that endures in every person. Dispel the confusions that cling close to my soul that I may see with eyes washed by your grace, that I may see myself and all people with eyes cleansed by the freshness of the new day's light (J. Philip Newell, *Celtic Benediction*, Canterbury Press, Norwich, 2000, p. 40).

Seeing people in this way is not a trick of the light; rather, it is a direct result of God helping us to see life more and more from his perspective. Without his help it is not something we naturally do. The apostle Paul described this new way of looking at people when he wrote, 'So from now on we regard no one from a worldly point of view. Though we once regarded Christ in this way, we do so no longer' (2 Corinthians 5:16). In other words, look for signs of God the Maker in every one of his creatures you meet.

Being a Christian should therefore enrich your relationships, but at the same time it should make you less dependent on the approval and acceptance of others – good though those things can be. I meet people of all ages whose sense of self-worth and value is entirely dependent on receiving praise from others. They find it hard to trust people, are disabled by any criticism and sense rejection when none is intended. Do you want to know how much you are worth? It is incredibly liberating to discover that God thought you were worth giving his Son for!

What about my family?

Your family may or may not welcome or understand the news that you have become a Christian. If they have not had any exposure to Christianity, or even spiritual issues generally, before now, do not be surprised if they are bemused by your apparent need for faith. They may even fear that you have become involved in some sort of sect or cult. You will need to reassure them that you are part of the mainstream Christian church. Give them time to adjust to the idea – remembering that your own discovery of faith has probably been a gradual journey.

If your family are part of another religious faith, they may well be experiencing a mixture of sadness, a sense of rejection and even anger. A friend of mine who is a British Asian Christian always stresses the point that having become a Christian does not mean that he has rejected his entire cultural heritage. His religious beliefs are different, but his dress, his taste in music and food and the values surrounding the family that his parents instilled in him reflect his cultural heritage.

Try to keep communication with them as open as possible. Do not let your involvement in a church squeeze them out through a lack of time. If this happens they will be understandably resentful!

Whatever your situation – whether you are still based in the family home or not – remember that the home is not the place for preaching sermons! One of the Ten Commandments in the Bible is 'Honour your father and mother.' This is not always easy, but continue to make it your aim. Accept that you will be misunderstood at times and perhaps hurt by how your family reacts to you. Continue to love them and be forgiving. In time, the way you act will be a far more effective message to them about God.

If that sounds a little negative, it is only because I want to be realistic. I know of many instances where one member of a family becoming a Christian has led in time to whole families discovering Jesus for themselves. Your family may become inquisitive and ask you questions about your faith, especially as they see it making a positive difference in your life. When they do, be honest about what you do and don't know. Talk about the things you find difficult and struggle with, as well as the exciting and positive things you see God doing in your life. You may think this strange advice – as though I was encouraging you to score an own goal in football. We are not meant to be spin-doctors for Jesus! A little girl asked her mum, 'Do all fairy stories begin "Once upon a time"? 'Oh, no,' replied her mum, 'Some begin "I became a Christian and all my problems disappeared"!' Your family will find your honesty believable. It may help them to see that faith is a possibility for people like them as well.

Pray for your family. Thank God for any and all of the positive things about your family and your upbringing. Ask him to help you to forgive anything that needs forgiving. Jesus knew what it was to be misunderstood by his own family. The Bible tells us that even his own brothers did not believe in him (John 7:5). As people started flocking to Jesus, his family decided that he'd lost his marbles and that they should take him into care (Mark 3:21). Jesus made it clear that our relationship with God should be our number one relationship, taking precedence even over family. However, even if the members of your family respond negatively to you, resist the temptation to write them off. When Jesus was being crucified he looked down from the cross, saw his watching mother and urged a close friend to look after her (John 19:26).

Is it OK to have friends who aren't Christians?

Absolutely yes! Much of what I wrote about your relationships with your family applies to your wider circle of friends. Friendships may change, but work hard at not getting cut off from your existing friends unless there are things about their lifestyle that are particularly destructive for you. For example, I can think of times when people who have been involved in crime or the drugs scene have needed to put some distance between themselves and their friends, for a time at least. These are the exceptions rather than the rule.

Your friends may react in a variety of ways. They may well be surprised! If they have preconceived ideas of what Christians are like, they may fear they will lose your friendship. You can be the person who breaks that negative image – although it will take time. Expect some banter from them. Try not to get defensive about this. A good rule of thumb is not to take yourself too seriously.

I have always been a keen sportsman. I am competitive and I love the camaraderie that goes with team sports. When I first became a Christian, I remember being apprehensive about how my friends and teammates would react. There was plenty of leg-pulling; while one or two remained negative, I can honestly say that I have never lost friends as a result of my faith. They adjusted to gradual changes in my life. While initially they did not understand why I would no longer get drunk after a game, they soon realized that I still enjoyed a laugh and a joke and the social side of sport. In time, I became less argumentative on the pitch without losing my competitive edge; I like to think that I became a better player as a result!

Christianity is very positive about friendship, so your faith should make you a better friend to others. Here are a few of the gems on friendship from a book in the Bible called Proverbs that is crammed with wisdom:

A friend loves at all times.
(Proverbs 17:17)

There is a friend who sticks closer than a brother.
(Proverbs 18:24)

Wounds from a friend can be trusted.
(Proverbs 27:6)

Having encouraged you not to lose touch with your existing friends, I now want to urge you to start to develop a friendship with one or two other Christians. Sticking with a sporting flavour: look out for people whose honesty and mutual encouragement will make them good training partners as you grow in faith.

I have one or two long-term friends who, I know, care for me to the extent that they will challenge me if they see me losing my edge. Indeed, my closest friend was literally a training partner, in our rugby-playing days. We ran together, lifted weights and made idiots of ourselves on rugby tours! When I got married I asked him to be my best man. He wanted to show our guests how much God had changed us both since school days. However, the illustrations that he used of my former behaviour could hardly be described as the highlight of the wedding as far as my mother-in-law was concerned!

Friendships like this take time to develop but are worth the effort involved in developing and maintaining them. A good first step is to ask God, 'To whom could I be such a friend?' Knowing people with whom you can talk freely, pray and study the Bible will be a major factor in growing in your relationship with Jesus.

How can I share my faith with others?

If you make a great discovery it's natural to be enthusiastic about it to others. Authentic Christianity is usually contagious – not in the sense of being an unwanted infection, but rather because most people who come to faith do so through contact with a friend or family member.

God wants us to share our faith with people. Jesus' first followers were ordinary fishermen. He told one of them called

Peter that he would turn him into 'a fisher of men'! Years later, Peter wrote to other Christians that they should 'always be prepared to give an answer to everyone who asks you to give the reason for the hope you have' (1 Peter 3:15). He went on to say that this should be done 'with gentleness and respect'. In other words, our lives should be attractive and intriguing to others.

This is why it is so important that you do not become cut off from people who are not yet Christians. There are many books and courses available aimed at helping Christians to build friendships with others. In so doing, they are trying to remedy the damage done by well-intentioned but defective teaching about the need to be separate from the world, combined with over-demanding church life. As someone just beginning to follow Jesus, determine to follow his example when it comes to friendship. Stay in contact with the needy, the non-religious and those whom others look down on. Make this a priority, even if it means being misunderstood by the traditional church.

This will involve giving them your time. Share activities together, but aim to become the sort of friend who takes an active part in setting the agenda for your friendship group. If you passively go along with the crowd you may find yourself in difficulty. Look for opportunities to introduce them to Christian friends. Be there for them when they have tough times and do not be judgmental of them. Ask for God's help, so that you can be living proof of Jesus' words 'I have come that they may have life, and have it to the full' (John 10:10).

Then, when the appropriate occasion arises, you will be able to talk to them about your Christian faith. Christians often call this 'evangelism', because it is sharing the 'evangel' (meaning literally 'good news') with others. You may find this to be quite easy and natural for you; if so, that really is good news, because most Christians find it very difficult to talk to other people about Jesus. That is why Nick Pollard, one of the authors of this book, has also written a book called *Evangelism Made Slightly Less Difficult* (IVP, 1997). I certainly recommend that you read it.

How will my faith affect my view of sex and marriage?

It should enhance it! Judging from the news-stands, internet and television schedules, Western society is completely preoccupied with sex. Indeed, you could be forgiven for thinking that sex is no more than the selfish pursuit of some sort of physical release, with varying degrees of pleasure according to your or a partner's ability to get the mechanics right. Sex is used to meet all sorts of needs, often in a casual way that leaves people feeling at best dissatisfied and at worst used and abused.

The Christian view of sex is altogether richer than that. Despite the exploitative efforts of the multi-million-pound sex industry, it is worth pointing out that members of the human race have been taking a great deal of pleasure from sex since time immemorial. This is because sex and sexuality form one of God's great gifts to humanity. There is so much more to it than just the sex act. The Bible includes some of the most beautiful erotic literature known to men and women. If you are unconvinced, I suggest you take yourself off to a quiet corner and read through the book in the Bible known as the Song of Songs.

Once your heartbeat has returned to normal, you might care to ask yourself why such a book is included in the Bible. The answer will take you much deeper into a proper understanding of sex and the place of marriage. Throughout the Bible, the language of love and intimacy between men and women is used to illustrate the lifelong, committed and intimate relationship God wants to have with the human race and with each of us in our own right.

At times in history the church has given the impression that sex is primarily to serve the function of reproduction – to perpetuate the human race. If this were the case, then surely it would have been a lot less complicated if we had been designed to reproduce like microscopic amoebae. Less complicated maybe, but a lot less fun! Imagine: 'Can't come to the phone right now; just heading off into the corner to subdivide myself into a family!'

So sex is something to be enjoyed, both in the intimate act of lovemaking within marriage and in the general relating of men and women in life. It is part of God's plan and design for living. The ideal pattern for how men and women should relate is set out early in the Bible. Men and women need each other. The two genders are of equal status, different in make-up and complementary in purpose. In Genesis chapter 2 it is explained that 'a man will leave his father and mother and be united to his wife, and they will become one flesh' (Genesis 2:24).

The norm is that a man and woman will form a lifelong marriage, and this is meant to be the basic building-block of society. Although this is the general norm, obviously not of all us find ourselves married. Whatever the reason for this may be, it is really important to know that our status before God and our own sense of self-worth are not dependent on being married or in an active sexual relationship. Sex is important, but whatever the latest late-night chat-show host may say, it is not the defining quality for being human.

How becoming a Christian affects your view and experience of sex will depend on your current situation and past experience. Do not let anyone give you the impression that sexual immorality is some kind of unforgivable sin – something that disqualifies you from being a loved member of God's family. At the same time, you should be aware that sex is far more than a physical act on a par with shaking hands. In sex you are meant to give something of yourself; it is emotional and spiritual. As such, sexual experiences have the potential to give us great physical pleasure and deep emotional fulfilment. This is why they can also leave us feeling frighteningly vulnerable and emotionally scarred.

It will take effort on your part, the support of friends and God's help if you want and need to change or break out of a pattern of sexual behaviour that is different from God's ideal of marriage. However, be encouraged – many of us have found it possible to start afresh in our relationships. You really can put your past behind you. This is one of those areas of life in which the words 'If anyone is in Christ, there is a new creation: the old has gone, the new has come!' (2 Corinthians 5:17) are a tremendous encouragement.

Years ago, on a chat show, a famous film star renowned for his romantic lead roles was asked for his definition of a great lover. He paused. The interviewer and studio audience eagerly anticipated some juicy revelation. His response was surprising then and is timely now. 'A great lover is someone who can satisfy one woman for her entire life.'

8

Sin, the world and the devil

Nick Pollard

Is there really a personal devil?

Some people find it hard to believe in the idea of a personal devil. How, in today's modern world, can we really believe that there is some red character with horns and a forked tail? But that is not how the Bible describes him. The fact that the world has made the devil into a humorous cartoon character does not mean that he doesn't really exist. Indeed, when we look at the suffering in the world, one might think that it is easier to believe in the existence of a devil than in the existence of a God of love. But the Bible tells us that both exist. There is a God – and there is also a devil. And the bad news is that the devil wants to stop us enjoying the good world that God created – indeed, the Bible says that he is like a hungry 'lion looking for someone to devour' (1 Peter 5:8). But the good news is that the destructive devil is nowhere near as powerful as the creator God who made us and wants the very best for us.

To give us a clearer idea of what the devil is like, let's look at a story in the Old Testament. The book of Job tells us how the devil tries to destroy the faith of the godly man Job. But it also tells us some of the ways in which the devil is limited, compared with God. Look at a few verses from chapter 1. Verse 7 tells us that the devil had been 'roaming through the earth'. That is, he can be in only one place at one time – unlike God, who is everywhere at once (the theological term for this is 'omnipresent'). Then, verse 10 tells us that God has 'put a hedge around him [Job]', so the devil can't harm him. That is, the devil's power is limited – unlike God, whose power is total (the theological term is 'omnipotent'). Finally, verse 11 tells us that the devil thinks that if all the good things Job has are taken away, Job will curse God. Read the rest of the book and you will find that the devil is wrong: Job will not curse God. So the devil does not know what will really happen – unlike God, who knows even the future (the theological term is 'omniscient').

Thus, although the devil is like a lion seeking to devour us, he is really more like a toothless lion: all roar and no power. Whereas God is omnipresent, omnipotent and omniscient, the devil is none of these. In fact, he is nothing like God at all. Whereas God always has existed and he created us all, the devil is just a created being – an angel who turned his back on God. Indeed, it seems that the greatest power the devil has comes from his ability to lie to us and to deceive us into thinking that he has more power than he has; that is why Jesus described him as a 'liar and the father of lies' (John 8:44).

The New Testament puts it even more clearly when it says that God has 'rescued us from the dominion of darkness' (Colossians 1:13) and that nothing, not even the devil, can separate us from the love of God (Romans 8:38–39).

What is sin?

Many people think that Christians believe in a God who is a boring old man in the sky, with a long grey beard, dressed in a Marks & Spencer nightie and surrounded by little fat babies. And what do they think that we believe this God does all day? He looks for ways of stopping us enjoying ourselves. So if God sees us having fun he says 'I'll soon stop that – I'll call that "sin".' That's why everything that's fun in this world is either illegal, immoral or fattening – and if it doesn't fit in one of those three categories, then it causes cancer in rats.

But, despite what they think, that isn't the God we really believe in; it is neither the God we see described in the Bible nor the God revealed in Jesus. Rather, we can see a God who created us to enjoy life; who says that he has given us all good things to enjoy (1 Timothy 6:17); and who told us through Jesus that he has come to give us life 'to the full' (John 10:10).

Because God wants us to enjoy life, he warns us against things that will harm us – it is these things that he calls 'sin'. Take a simple thing like a microphone, for example. We can know how to use a microphone because it comes with a set of instructions – the manufacturer tells us how to use it, so that we can enjoy it and benefit from it. But imagine that we decide not to follow the maker's instructions. Suppose that we decide that we want to use the microphone for something else: perhaps as a hammer to knock in nails. The fact is, we could do that – but the microphone would very soon break, because it is not designed for that purpose. That is rather like sin. Sin is refusing to obey the maker's instructions – using your body or mind or spirit for something for which it is not designed. And why is God so opposed to sin? Because he knows that it will harm you and others.

You see, sin damages us and separates us. If I sin against a friend of mine (perhaps I lie to him or steal from him), then I will find that there is a barrier in my relationship with him. The next time we are together I will feel awkward in his presence – my sin has separated me from him. In rather the same way, sin separates us from God. But the good news is that God wants to restore us into a proper relationship with him; he wants us to be forgiven. That is why he came to earth in the person of Jesus: to die for us – to take the separation from God that is due to us – so that we may come back into a proper relationship with him.

What do I do if I sin as a Christian?

Becoming a Christian means being forgiven for our sin. That doesn't mean just that we are forgiven for the sins we have committed until then; it means entering into a state of forgiveness where we are forgiven for *all* our sins – past, present and future. It means knowing that, whatever we do, we are forgiven because Jesus died for us and we are trusting in his death to pay the price for all our sins.

Unfortunately, I meet many Christians who haven't really understood this. They believe that God has forgiven them for their sins in the past, but they are not really sure that God will keep on forgiving them for sins in the present or future.

When people struggle with this I usually invite them to look with me at 1 John 1:9. This promises us that, if we confess our sins, he is faithful and just and will forgive us our sins. Notice, then, that God forgives us because he is 'just', not because he is 'merciful'.

This is important. It's a bit like a chocoholic I know. She is pretty much addicted to chocolate: she doesn't just drop the odd tab of chocolate – more like mainline injections of chocolate sauce. She is also quite scatty and forgetful. Imagine that one day she goes into a shop to get some chocolate. She takes it off the shelf and stands in the checkout queue. But she can't resist it; before she gets to the till she has already eaten it all. Then she realizes that she hasn't got any money on her – so she smiles sweetly at the shopkeeper and says sorry; she asks him to forgive her. If he is merciful, he might do that. But imagine she does it again the next day – would he forgive her again? Perhaps he might, but he wouldn't do it a third time or a fourth. That is the problem with mercy – it might run out. Is that what God is like?

Does he forgive us because he is merciful? Might he decide that enough is enough and he doesn't want to forgive us any more?

The fact is that God does not forgive us because he is merciful; as it says in 1 John 1:9, he forgives us because he is just. Let's come back to the illustration. Imagine I know what my friend is like, so I go to the shopkeeper and give him a blank cheque. I tell him that I will pay her bill: I say, 'Whatever chocolate she takes, just charge it to my cheque.' Then, when she asks him to forgive her, he has to – not because he is being merciful but because of justice. The price has been paid; he has to forgive her.

That is rather like what Jesus did on the cross. He paid the price for your and my sin – so God forgives you not because he is being merciful to you, but because God is a God of justice, and the price has already been paid by Jesus.

Can we always be forgiven for every sin?

Jesus said, 'Truly I tell you, people will be forgiven all their sins and all the blasphemies they utter' (Mark 3:28). Whatever we do, if we have repented and are placing our faith in Jesus' death to pay the price for our sin, then we can be sure that we are forgiven. He said that all sins and all blasphemies will be forgiven. So it seems that there is nothing that we can do that cannot be forgiven.

However, in the very next verse (Mark 3:29) Jesus says that 'whoever blasphemes against the Holy Spirit will never be forgiven, but is guilty of an eternal sin.' Many new Christians have their new life in Christ blighted by the fear that they may have committed this unforgivable sin. But they have always misunderstood what Jesus meant. As with every verse of the Bible, to understand it we have to read it in its context. Jesus said this in response to people who were rejecting him so strongly that they even thought he was acting by the power of the devil (Mark 3:30). This unforgivable sin, then, is a state of total and utter rejection of Jesus. So of course one cannot be forgiven for that sin – because to be forgiven we have to accept Jesus and his sacrifice on the cross for us. The unforgivable sin is refusing to come to Jesus to accept the forgiveness he offers because we reject him totally and utterly. But Jesus wants everyone to come to him to receive forgiveness. Those who reject him can repent and accept him; that is what the gospel message is all about. So, this unforgivable sin is not a once-off sin; it is, as Jesus put it, 'an eternal sin'. It is not a sin that you 'may have committed in the past' – it is a present, ongoing sin of rejecting Jesus so entirely that you refuse to accept the forgiveness he offers. In such a situation the person cannot receive forgiveness. The young Christians who have been worried whether they may have committed this sin (mistakenly thinking it is some past sin) are clearly not in this state. If they were committing the unforgivable sin of continuing to totally and utterly reject Jesus, then they would not be worried about his forgiveness!

Does that mean that I can do whatever I like and still be forgiven?

It does mean that, if we have truly repented and are trusting in Jesus for the forgiveness of our sins, then we will always be forgiven. But that, in turn, means that we won't want to sin.

If we have repented we will want to do what Jesus wants – we will want to follow him. And if we are trusting in Jesus' death for our forgiveness, we will realize how much it cost Jesus to pay the price for our sin – so we will not want to commit more sins.

The Bible puts it this way: 'No one who lives in him keeps on sinning. No one who continues to sin has either seen him or known him' (1 John 3:6). But that doesn't mean that we won't sin; we will, because we are imperfect human people. But we won't want to – we will want to follow Jesus; we will want to do what is right, even though we do still sin. The Bible describes it like this: 'I have the desire to do what is good, but I cannot carry it out. For I do not do the good I want to do, but the evil I do not want to do

– this I keep on doing. Now if I do what I do not want to do, it is no longer I who do it, but it is sin living in me that does it' (Romans 7:18–20). That is why we need the forgiveness that Jesus provides to rescue us from the consequence of this sin – 'Who will rescue me from this body of death? Thanks be to God, who delivers me through Jesus Christ our Lord!' (Romans 7:24–25).

9

God

Paul Harris

Can God be known?

Over the years many people have told me the story of their spiritual journey. They have described the discovery of knowing Jesus Christ in a way that has radically altered their life. Many of them have wrestled intellectually and emotionally with the idea of becoming a Christian for weeks or months, before praying a simple prayer – 'God, if you are real – I want to know you.' That has usually signalled the end of the struggle and preceded a more articulate prayer of trust and commitment. It is a prayer that begs one of the deepest questions in life. Can God be known?

Many people come to the conclusion that there must be something – someone or some force – behind life and the world of nature. This first cause, force, thing or person must, by definition, be in a class of their own and unlike anything or anyone we know. We need a unique descriptive term, so we will give it/him/her a code name: 'god'. The apparent thought and purpose in nature leads to what is known as the 'argument from design' for the existence of God. The next question is the one we are addressing. It is one thing to decide there must have been a god behind life, but is this god still around to be known in any meaningful sense?

One of the most influential early Christians was someone called Paul. He played a key role in helping the revolutionary message about Jesus spread beyond Israel and Palestine. Although he was not one of Jesus' original followers, he was a contemporary and eventual colleague of Jesus' closest friends: men such as Peter, James and John. His epistles (letters) make up a large part of the second main section of the Bible.

Coming from a strict and traditional Jewish background, he was a fierce persecutor of the early Christians. Thinking he was serving God by crushing this new movement that was springing up, he was on his way to Damascus when he had a life-changing encounter with God. In a vision, he believed he saw and heard Jesus speaking to him, challenging him over what he was doing. His life was changed, literally in a flash. From then on he committed himself to spreading the life-changing message of Jesus. (You can read an account of how Paul met Jesus in Acts 9 and his own account in Acts 26.)

Paul was the ideal person to communicate the Christian message across cultures. His family background and education had also given him experience and understanding of the Greek and Roman cultures of his day. He is a good example of what we should aim to be – a world Christian: someone with wide horizons and in touch with the culture of our day.

Paul's travels took him to Athens. It was a real hotbed of religion, spirituality and superstition. People there were fascinated by any new teaching and belief, however wild or wacky! If you have ever been to a new age or psychic fair, or wandered down the High Street of Glastonbury in England, you will have some idea of the flavour of the place! Paul was sad to see the crazy stuff people were prepared to hitch their lives to.

He noticed that among all the shrines and altars to different idols there was even one dedicated to 'An Unknown God'. Talk about hedging your bets! Paul took his opportunity and dived into the debate. He declared that he was going to introduce his listeners to the Living and Knowable God. He argued that God was the Creator; that he was the God of history; and that he did not live in temples that men and women had built. In touch with the culture of the day, Paul quoted from some contemporary poets. He went on to say that God had revealed himself, so that people 'would seek him and perhaps reach out for him and find him, though he is not far from any one of us. "For in him we live and move and have our being."' In other words, Paul declared 'God is knowable!' His message went down a storm with some and kicked up a storm with others. It is a dramatic account – you can read it for yourself in Acts 17.

A high-profile pagan web site has in its introduction on the home page the declaration that pagans hold diverse views, but that they are united in worshipping the great 'Unknowable Spirit'. New age – same challenge!

Jesus was very clear on the question of knowing God. In his day many spiritual seekers were looking for what they termed 'eternal life'. Words from a prayer Jesus prayed towards the end of his life, which is recorded in John chapter 17, show clearly what he understood by eternal life. 'Now this is eternal life: that they know you, the only true God, and Jesus Christ, whom you have sent' (verse 3).

Countless gurus and prophets since have offered their take on the way to eternity. Cosmetic surgeons make a pretty profit from people who want the appearance of eternal youth. If it's eternal life you want, then Jesus' words have timeless appeal and effect. Get to know Jesus and you get to know God! (See John 14:7.)

What is God like?

As soon as we use the term 'God is like' we are in danger of falling into idolatry: that is, reducing God to resemble an invention of our own imagination. God, being God, is at one and the same time knowable and yet beyond our comprehension. If my mind could grasp all there is to know about God, what would that make me?

During my teens I would hold forth on all sorts of topics – a definite case of the 'hire a teenager while they still know everything' syndrome! In a valiant attempt to bring some sense of perspective, my father would regularly inform me that 'God made man in his image and unfortunately man returns the compliment!' Words from the Bible spell it out more plainly.

'For my thoughts are not your thoughts,
   neither are your ways my ways,'
               declares the LORD.
'As the heavens are higher than the earth,
   so are my ways higher than your ways
   and my thoughts than your thoughts.'
(Isaiah 55:8–9)

God has given you a brain, so use it well – but recognize your limits!

As a student I used to spend holidays working as a porter in a large hospital in Slough. One afternoon I was asked to transfer an old man from Accident & Emergency to the Psychiatric Department. As soon as I appeared in the door to his cubicle, the little old fellow in the wheelchair exclaimed 'Gabriel, thank goodness you're here – these nurses won't believe I'm God!' I have been mistaken for all sorts of people over the years, but never the archangel Gabriel! 'God' being deemed not a danger, I set off down the long corridors pushing him in his wheelchair. Two rather large young ladies were approaching and as we passed them 'God' exclaimed, 'Cor! Gabriel, look at the size of them!' A moment later, he looked up over his shoulder and said, 'Sometimes I wonder if I really am God – 'cos if I was I wouldn't say things like that, would I?'

When someone makes claims about their identity or their ability, we observe their behaviour to see whether the walk matches the talk. At least my wheelchair-bound 'God' was able to recognize that he might not be the full deal!

Over the years people have wished they could see God. Seeing would be believing – or so they have claimed. If only he was someone like us it would be so much simpler. Here is where Jesus comes in. Effectively God says, 'If you want to know what I'm like – look at my Son!' We see this expressed from Jesus' perspective. His disciples were struggling with this same question of what God is like. One of them, called Philip, said, 'Lord, show us the Father and that will be enough for us.' Jesus replied, 'Anyone who has seen me has seen the Father.' (Read this in John 14, verse 5 onwards.) This is one of a number of occasions on which Jesus spelt out that he was God. It's worth knowing about, since sooner or later you will meet someone who will argue that Jesus was a great teacher but that he never himself claimed to be divine!

Is God all-knowing?

There are a number of incidents recorded showing that Jesus knew exactly what people he met were thinking – times when he understood the real nature of a problem better than someone who had approached him for help. At the time of writing a television series is running that features a man who appears to be able to read people's minds. If he met me it would be a case of 'What's the trick?' or 'I hope he can't *really* read my mind!'

One hot, dusty day at high noon, Jesus encountered a woman by a well. She was a total stranger. His opening gambit was to ask for a drink of water, and before long they were talking theology. Suddenly Jesus revealed that he knew precisely all about her complicated marital and sexual history. Enough to make anyone run a mile; but in her case it was the clincher. She set off round the town inviting all and sundry to meet Jesus with these words:

'Come, see a man who told me everything I ever did. Could this be the Messiah?' I am not sure that would have been my first reaction! See what you think by reading it for yourself, in John chapter 4.

This divine, supernatural knowledge certainly gave Jesus the edge over his opponents. However hard they tried to catch him out or trap him with trick questions, he was one step ahead. Matthew chapter 22 has some splendid examples of this. Knowledge like this certainly adds to your performance if you are a teacher; no surprise, therefore, that in the teaching stakes Jesus was in a league of his own. Matthew records that 'the crowds were amazed at his teaching, because he taught as one who had authority, and not as their teachers of the law'(Matthew 7:28–29).

Is God really the Creator?

Jesus' authority extended to the field of nature. He was able to operate within what we call 'the laws of nature' in a way that was clearly supernatural. One night he and his disciples were crossing the Sea of Galilee in a small boat. Jesus was catching up on some sleep when a storm blew up. Despite the fact that a number of them were experienced local fishermen, his disciples were scared and convinced that their number was up. They shook Jesus awake and then were themselves shaken, when his word of command to the winds and the waves produced an instant response! (Read more about this incident in Luke chapter 8, from verse 22.)

Later in his life, Jesus' close friend John reflected on these events and realized that the explanation for Jesus being able to control the elements, walk on water, heal the sick, raise the dead and turn water into wine lay in the fact that he had been intimately involved in the very act of creation. John was inspired to write that the Word – another name for Jesus – 'was with God in the beginning. Through him all things were made; without him nothing was made that has been made.' You can read this in John chapter 1.

If you are from a scientific background, the idea of a Creator God may be difficult to reconcile with what you have previously been taught. I remember from my school days a science teacher who was adamant that faith and science were incompatible. It seemed to be the central tenet of his personal beliefs; I suspect that, over the years, countless young people have bought this line without stopping to think it through for themselves.

A university student once declared to me in a question-and-answer session 'I don't believe in God; I believe in evolution,' as though these were two logical and mutually exclusive explanations of life. If he visited the church we attended for seven years in Southampton, he would meet among the members thirty or more medical doctors and a similar number of research scientists and professors from the Science faculties of the University. These are all women and men whose various studies of the observable scientific processes in the natural world have led them to search for and believe in God the Creator.

Is God subject to limits?

God's authority is absolute and without limit. This is often described as his sovereignty. He is sovereign. He is answerable to no-one, because there is no higher authority. He needs no assistance. Although he takes pleasure in our worship and devotion, he is in no way dependent on our, or anyone else's, approval. If no-one ever prayed to him or worshipped him, he would not be booking into a celebrity clinic with an identity crisis – no 'sometimes I wonder if I really am God' moments for him!

In Jesus' life this authority was seen to extend beyond the physical, natural world into the spiritual realm. In his time, as today, many were gripped by fear and superstition. Occult and dark influences destroyed people's lives. He confronted the presence and evidence of demonic power in people's lives with complete command. Matthew recorded a clear example, and the effect it had on those who witnessed it, in chapter 8 of his account of Jesus' life.

It is a sad reality that today, for all our technological sophistication, many people are scarred by events and actions that we can describe and explain only in terms of outright evil. In 1996 people across the world were shocked by the indiscriminate shooting of children in a school in Dunblane, Scotland. In the aftermath, the words of the impressive head teacher were widely reported: 'Yesterday evil visited us.'

Jesus never denied the reality of evil, nor minimized the extent of people's suffering. He was completely up front with his disciples on these issues. Among his last words to them he said 'In this world you will have trouble. But take heart! I have overcome the world' (John 16:33).

Is God forgiving?

Jesus scandalized people by speaking and acting in a way that left them in no doubt that he thought he was God. The clearest example of this was the way in which he offered and declared forgiveness to the sinners and outcasts who seemed to be drawn to him like moths to a flame. In one of his earliest healing miracles he enabled a paralysed man to walk and told him his sins were forgiven. Watching religious leaders were outraged: 'He's blaspheming! Who can forgive sins but God alone?' (See Mark chapter 2 for the full account.)

Forgiveness was central to Jesus' mission. For him, forgiveness was not a one-off act. Forgiveness was a state of mind – something he took every opportunity to declare and to demonstrate, right to the end of his life on earth. Even when nailed to a cross, he asked God to forgive his enemies and executioners! People who were crucified often used their last moments to vent their anger and agony in abusing the crowd. Jesus, by contrast, prayed 'Father, forgive them, for they do not know what they are doing' (Luke 23:34).

He offered forgiveness and hope to a penitent thief who was being crucified alongside him. It is a matter of supreme irony that when he was in the very act of dying to save the world, onlookers mocked him, saying, 'He saved others; let him save himself if he is God's Messiah, the Chosen One' (Luke 23:35).

The way Jesus conducted himself in death had such an impact on the battle-hardened centurion responsible for overseeing the execution that he was moved to praise God and recognize that Jesus was a genuinely righteous man (Luke 23:47). Men and women through the years have been so moved by the account of Jesus' death that it has changed their lives too. On Good Friday 1972, an arrogant and confused teenager who had been challenged to take the claims of Jesus on his life seriously locked his bedroom door and read the account of Jesus' life and death. He never reached the happy ending of the resurrection, when Jesus was raised to life. The account of Jesus' death was enough to make him kneel down by his bed and, with tears streaming down his face, ask for forgiveness. I was that teenager, and that moment changed the course of my life. Do not attempt to live as a follower of Jesus unless you know deep in your very being that God is forgiving!

Is God loving?

If Jesus' mission was forgiveness, what was his motivation? Motives matter in life. Sooner or later, for better or worse they are always revealed. You do not have to look for long at the accounts of Jesus' life before his motivation becomes apparent. Arguably the best-known Bible verse – John 3:16 – spells out the driving force and defining feature of Jesus' life and mission. Simply put, it was love. 'God so loved the world that he gave his one and only Son, that whoever believes in him shall not perish but have eternal life.'

Love was central to Jesus' life because it is central to the character of God. Jesus was obedient to his Father's will and purpose not because he was a pre-programmed automaton, but because of love. He acted not from a sense of duty but freely, as an expression and natural outworking of his Father's love for him. 'Very truly I tell you,' he said, 'the Son can do nothing by himself; he can do only what he sees his Father doing, because whatever the Father does the Son also does. For the Father loves the Son and shows him all he does' (John 5:19–20). A case of 'like father, like son' on a cosmic scale!

John was inspired to write on another occasion: 'God is love. This is how God showed his love among us: he sent his one and only Son into the world that we might live through him. This is love: not that we loved God, but that he loved us and sent his Son as an atoning sacrifice for our sins.' John goes on to say that it therefore follows that love should be a hallmark of Christian faith. Love should characterize all the Christian's relationships. (You can read this for yourself in 1 John 4:7 onwards – that is, his letter near the end of the Bible – easily confused with his Gospel, which comes earlier!)

What is the Holy Trinity?

Sooner or later you will come across this phrase: 'the Holy Trinity'. You might see it on a church notice board; but you won't find it in the Bible – well, not in as many words! It is an important term in the vocabulary of theologians, but don't be frightened of it. Some years ago there was a film called *Nuns on the Run*, in which two small-time criminals hid in a convent school by posing as nuns. The biggest challenge they faced was explaining the Holy Trinity to a class of teenage girls!

The term describes a profound and paradoxical feature of God, whom you are getting to know. Whenever I come across an apparent contradiction or paradox to do with God, I think I should take off my intellectual shoes, metaphorically speaking, as it usually means I am about to venture onto holy ground. Christianity is a monotheist religion. Like Islam and Judaism, it speaks of there being only one God, as opposed to lots of competing or complementary gods (polytheism). However, a distinctive and central Christian belief is that God shows himself and works in such a way that he is most fully described as being three persons in one. You see what I mean about paradox!

The way God operates and relates to his creation, including human beings, leads us to describe him as God the Father, God the Son (that is, Jesus) and God the Holy Spirit (sometimes referred to as the Holy Ghost, meaning spirit). This is not a gang of gods! God does not have a split personality – he is indivisible. So why three persons, you might reasonably ask?

People use many analogies to cast light on this aspect of God's nature. They may be helpful to a degree; but remember that, like all analogies, they are not the whole story.

Probably the most important points to grasp at this stage, in the light of the earlier section 'Can God be known?' are that:

1. God is personal, as opposed to an impersonal life force.
2. Personhood and relationship are central to the character and nature of God.

I said that you do not find the Holy Trinity in so many words in the Bible. You may meet members of other religions or quasi-Christian sects who will tell you that the Trinity cannot be found in the Bible. You need to know why that is not true. Here are three places where God the Holy Trinity can be clearly seen.

God the Holy Trinity is seen in the creation
Genesis chapter 1 verse 26 says 'Then God said, let us make man [that is, the human race, male and female] in our image'. To

whom was God speaking? His articulated thoughts or words are part of the creative act – whatever view of creation you take in terms of time and process. This is the divine conception behind creation. Verse 2 of the same opening chapter says, 'the Spirit of God was hovering over the waters.'

John begins his life story of Jesus by painting the big picture. Referring to Jesus as the Word (remember what I said above about God *speaking* the world into being), he says that Jesus was in the beginning with God and was God. He did not come into being at a later stage. He then says: 'Through him all things were made; without him nothing was made that has been made.' (Read it yourself in John chapter 1.)

God the Holy Trinity is seen in the baptism of Jesus

After a mostly normal childhood and his emergence through teenage years into adulthood, Jesus set about doing the work that he had come to earth to do. This is described as his public ministry. The impact he made was the result of just three years' work! As he began this last and most important chapter of his life, there was an event that shows God as the Holy Trinity most clearly. As part of his final preparations Jesus was baptized, to demonstrate his solidarity with people who wanted to be clean and to make a fresh start. He did this even though he had lived a perfect holy life focused on God his father! It was a remarkable event in which God spoke and acted in a powerful and tangible way. It is recorded in the first chapter of Mark's account of Jesus' life: 'As Jesus was coming up out of the water, he saw heaven being torn open and the Spirit descending on him like a dove. And a voice came from heaven: "You are my Son, whom I love; with you I am well pleased." ' (See Mark 1:10–11.)

There you see God the Father, Son and Holy Spirit acting and interacting simultaneously and with unity of purpose. This always reminds me of the times in the old Tom and Jerry cartoons when Spike the bulldog puffs up his chest, looks at his young pup and says 'That's my boy!' Profound stuff.

God the Holy Trinity is seen in the teaching and prayers of Jesus
As Jesus was nearing the end of his life on earth he prepared his disciples for the time when they would no longer see him physically. He promised that he would never leave them alone. In John chapters 14, 15 and 16 he talks explicitly about asking his Father to send the Holy Spirit:

> And I will ask the Father, and he will give you another advocate to help you and be with you for ever – the Spirit of truth (John 14:16).

> the Holy Spirit, whom the Father will send in my name, will teach you all things (John 14:26).

> All that belongs to the Father is mine. That is why I said the Spirit will receive from me what he will make known to you (John 16:15).

God the Holy Spirit is clearly described by Jesus himself. The key thing is to remember how this reveals the personal nature of the God who made you; whom you can know through Jesus and serve because the Holy Spirit is living in you. Do not get hung up trying to understand every facet of this deep mystery. Try to avoid being like the apocryphal young preacher who, having taken too much whisky to calm his nerves, described God the Holy and Indivisible Trinity as 'Big Daddy, Junior and the Spook'!

Why God the Father?

Christians have traditionally referred to God as Father. Even before Jesus the Son of God came to earth the Jewish scriptures, our Old Testament, referred to God in this way (Deuteronomy 32:6 and Isaiah 9:6 are two good examples). The best-known Christian prayer is the Lord's Prayer – a form and pattern of prayer that Jesus personally taught his disciples. It continues to be used throughout the world and across cultures and begins 'Our Father in heaven'. The advent and acceptance of feminism has understandably caused people to question whether using the male term 'Father' is simply an unfortunate example of male supremacy, reflecting Christianity's roots in a patriarchal society. Does this mean that God is male?

God is totally other. He is neither male nor female, but divine. His character or image was reflected in the human race being created male and female. 'Father' and 'he' are used to express and emphasize personhood rather than gender. We spell 'Father' with a capital letter to stress that this is a divine title and to express reverence. The 'parent' title reflects the creative and ongoing nurturing activity of God.

In Western society many people associate the word 'father' with, at best, an absent figure and at worst, an abuser. This has been a further challenge to the use of the term. Do not lose sight of the main issue here. In Jesus you have a relationship with God who gave you life and who nurtures you. God can be the parent that some of us never had – always loving, always present. Look at what your Heavenly Parent says:

'Can a mother forget the baby at her breast
    and have no compassion for the child she has borne?
Though she may forget,
    I will not forget you!'
(Isaiah 49:15)

Elsewhere in the Bible, female imagery and language are used to describe how God relates to us. For example, in his desire to protect us God is described as a mother hen (Matthew 23:37).

Why a Son who dies?

In early 2004 cinema audiences throughout the world were transfixed by Mel Gibson's graphic film *The Passion of the Christ*. The film left a deep and lasting impression on people who were confronted, many for the first time, with the bloody violence surrounding the last hours of Jesus' life on earth. They realized, as I had back in 1972 (see the section 'Is God forgiving?'), that a real man had been subjected to extreme cruelty before dying an excruciating death.

It is a central belief of the Christian faith that Jesus' death was far more than an inspiring example of forgiveness and bravery. In his death Jesus was literally receiving the death sentence due to each and every member of the human race on account of the sin and self-centredness in all our lives. Jesus' death had timeless and cosmic significance. In God's overall scheme of things, he had chosen this as the great act of reconciliation. The great early church leader Paul explained it to Christians in Rome like this: 'You see, at just the right time, when we were still powerless, Christ died for the ungodly ... But God demonstrates his own love for us in this: while we were still sinners, Christ died for us' (Romans 5:6, 8).

You may feel uncomfortable with the idea of God showing his love to you and me by sacrificing his Son. Most of us would not warm to someone who sacrifices their child for someone else. Surely the child should have a say in it? If we judge God by human standards on this issue, we miss two key points.

First, Jesus had the choice to cooperate with his Father's plan. His was not an automated response, but rather a conscious, unselfish act of loving obedience.

The second point is the all-important fact of the resurrection. During his life Jesus repeatedly expressed his belief that, even if his enemies killed him, God his Father would bring him back to life. 'He [Jesus] then began to teach them that the Son of Man [one of his favourite titles for himself] must suffer many things ... and that he must be killed and after three days rise again' (Mark 8:31). To his opponents this was nonsensical madness or blasphemy. Jesus clearly linked his claims to divinity to resurrection. It would be the ultimate vindication.

The early Christians were equally adamant that Jesus' resurrection not only gave them hope of life after death, but was the proof positive that Jesus was all that he had claimed to be. Paul was typically categorical when he was inspired to write, 'if Christ has not been raised, our preaching is useless and so is your faith' (1 Corinthians 15:14).

What about the Holy Spirit?

You may be wondering what the Holy Spirit does. When you made the decision to become a follower of Jesus, you received the Holy Spirit. That fact is spelled out in Acts 2, where the first Christian sermon is recorded. A recently failed follower of Jesus, called Peter, preached an inspired sermon and a large number of his hearers became convinced that Jesus was the Son of God. They knew this must have personal implications for them and asked, 'What shall we do?' Peter replied: 'Repent and be baptized, every one of you, in the name of Jesus Christ for the forgiveness of your sins. And you will receive the gift of the Holy Spirit' (Acts 2:38).

In other words, God is in your life. The Holy Spirit helps you to know Jesus in a real and intimate way. He makes you more like Jesus, changing you over a lifetime so that you can become the woman or man that God made you to be. The Holy Spirit inspires you to pray, helps you to understand the Bible and gives you gifts and abilities to use to serve God and your fellow human beings.

God the Holy Spirit enables ordinary people like you and me to live extraordinary lives. Paul, whom we were thinking about earlier, prayed for close friends that they would be 'filled to the measure of all the fullness of God' (Ephesians 3:19). Get into the good habit of beginning each day by thanking God for Jesus and the gift of the Holy Spirit. Ask to be filled again with the Spirit, ready to tackle the challenges and opportunities of the day in such a way as will help other people to see Jesus in you.

10

The Bible

Nick Pollard

Why is the Bible so important?

Claire was a young Christian who hardly ever read the Bible. 'I don't need to,' she said, 'I just listen to Jesus and follow him.' That sounds great – but it is extremely dangerous. It is true that Jesus does speak to us in many different ways: through situations and circumstances; through other people; even directly, through thoughts in our minds. But how will we know whether that really is Jesus speaking? The Bible is the most trustworthy authority for helping us to discern what is from God and what is just our own wishful thinking.

The fact is that the one way we can be certain that God will speak to us is through the Bible. Claire wanted to listen to Jesus and to follow him. The best way to listen to Jesus is to read what he said, recorded for us in the Bible; and the best way to follow him is to respond to his teaching and example, recorded for us in the Bible.

A student called Adrian asked, 'How can you base your life on a stuffy old book like the Bible?' The answer is that it depends what that book is. If it is simply a stuffy old book, then it would be mad to take it so seriously. But if it really is God's word to us, the means through which our Creator speaks to us, then it would be mad to ignore it. So which is it – a stuffy old book or God's word?

There is a great deal of evidence for the historical reliability of the Bible. It was written down by witnesses or on the first-hand account of eyewitnesses. Archaeological evidence confirms the accuracy of their record. And the existence of early manuscript copies shows that the text has been transmitted reliably through the centuries.

If we can thus be sure that the Bible is reliable history, we can then consider whether it is God's word. The four Gospels (Matthew, Mark, Luke and John) contain a record of Jesus' words. In them Jesus claims to be God become man – and proves his claim through his miracles (particularly rising from the dead). So, if Jesus really is God, and if the Gospels record his words, then we have in the Bible the words of God – God himself speaking.

Now we can look backwards from the Gospels. Jesus treats the Old Testament (the first and oldest part of the Bible, the bit that the Jewish people and Christians share) as the word of God. He submits himself to Scripture; he says explicitly of the Psalms (a book of ancient hymns and songs in the Old Testament) that David was speaking 'by the Holy Spirit' (Mark 12:36); and he calls the Old Testament law (the rules for living that God gave the Jewish people) 'the word of God' (Matthew 15:6). Then we can look forwards from the Gospels. Jesus predicts that God will speak to the disciples through his Holy Spirit, who will 'teach you all things and will remind you of everything I have said to you' (John 14:26). This teaching was then written down for us as the New Testament (the newer part of the Bible, which consists of a set of books written soon after Jesus lived).

If the Bible really is God's word to us – if he really will speak to us through it – then it must be really important. Claire and Adrian realized that, eventually – as I believe we all must.

What is in the Bible?

The Bible is a collection of sixty-six books, written by some forty different authors over several hundred years. Yet all of it was inspired by God – that is, he caused it to be written in such a way that he speaks to us through it.

The Bible is divided into two parts, called Testaments. The Old Testament is thirty-nine books that tell the story of the Jewish people leading up to Jesus, and how they related to the rest of the world. The New Testament is twenty-seven books which tell the story of Jesus' life and what has followed and will follow it. So, although it is only the four Gospels that tell the life and teaching of Jesus, the whole Bible focuses on him.

God speaks to us in different ways through the different styles of writing in the different parts of the Bible. Through poetic picture language God speaks to us symbolically. When poetic books say that 'the trees of the field shall clap their hands', God is using figurative language; he wants us to understand the under-lying message without taking the text literally. But then, through the historical books, God tells us exactly what happened at that time. When the Gospels record that Jesus walked on water, healed the sick and rose from the dead, God is giving us real history (read the beginning of Luke's Gospel and see how reliably Luke did his historical investigation) – so they are meant to be taken literally. Through didactic (direct teaching) language God tells us how he intends us to live. When the epistles (letters) show us how we can grow in our faith, God is teaching us what to do – and calling us to follow him.

How is the Bible relevant today?

The Bible was written many years ago, by people who were living in a particular cultural context. This means that the words were written in relation to that time and place. However, God inspired the writers in such a way that the words they wrote would be God's word to all people at all times in all places. This means that when we read the ancient songs of praise in the Old Testament we can identify with the words and make them our songs of praise. When we read the letters written to people in the churches in the New Testament we can see parallels with our own church life and learn the same lessons for ourselves. When we read the stories about Jesus' life we grow in understanding of what kind of person Jesus was and why he made such an impact, and why we too want to follow him.

Sometimes the Bible appears to cover specific issues that are not relevant today, and not to cover specific issues that are relevant today. When the Bible covers specific issues that are not relevant today, you will find that the general principles behind them will still be highly relevant. For example, the whole of chapter 8 of the book called 1 Corinthians (Paul's first letter to the church in Corinth) considers whether or not a Christian should eat food that has been sacrificed to idols (false gods made by men and women). I very much doubt that you will face this dilemma. It was a particular issue for those people at that time. However, there are principles there that will apply to you. When people at that time ate food that had been sacrificed to idols, they were usually considered to be publicly identifying with idol worship. The food itself wouldn't harm them at all, and there was really no problem with eating it – but other Christians who did not realize this and saw them apparently identifying with idol worship might find that their faith was harmed. There are plenty of activities today that are not in themselves inherently evil, but are usually considered to be a way of publicly identifying with ungodly behaviour. Applying the principles of this passage, it would be better not to do them if doing them meant that other Christians might find their faith was harmed.

Similarly, when the Bible doesn't appear to cover issues that are relevant today, you will find that it does still contain general principles that enable us to consider the specific issues. For example, a major question facing our culture today concerns the advances that are taking place in genetic manipulation. Is it right or wrong to engineer a human embryo in order to obtain stem cells from it; or to design a particular type of baby? The Bible does not tell us God's specific will regarding this – not surprising, if you consider when it was written. But it does contain a lot of general information about the value of individual life, even when it is unborn (see, for example, Psalm 139:13–16). This general information can help us as we seek to know God's will for such specific situations.

How will reading the Bible help me?

Young babies cannot survive unless they have food and drink. Then, as they grow, they need to be taught and trained. Finally, as they become increasingly active, they need light so they can see their way. In rather the same way, young Christians need to grow – and the Bible provides the same kind of help.

The Bible is food and drink to a Christian. The Old Testament says 'When your words came, I ate them; they were my joy and my heart's delight' (Jeremiah 15:16). Similarly, the New Testament tells us to 'crave pure spiritual milk, so that by it you may grow up in your salvation' (1 Peter 2:2). If you stop taking in physical food and drink, you will soon collapse and die. In the same way, all Christians need to feed on God's word in order to stay alive spiritually.

The Bible provides teaching and training for a Christian. It says, 'All scripture is God-breathed and is useful for teaching, rebuking, correcting and training in righteousness, so that all God's people may be thoroughly equipped for every good work' (2 Timothy 3:16–17). If you want to learn how to program a computer or to repair a car, you will need some kind of instruction manual to teach you. If you want to grow and develop in your faith you will need God's instruction manual – the Bible.

Lastly, the Bible provides guidance and direction. One of the Psalms says 'Your word is a lamp to my feet and a light for my path' (Psalm 119:105). If you want to know the way that you should go, the decisions you should take – and you feel that the way ahead is dark and unclear – then you need to read the Bible to shed God's light on your problem. When I have faced difficult decisions I have so often found that reading the Bible has enabled me to understand the right thing to do.

Which translation of the Bible should I use?

There is one original Bible – the collection of the original books written down by the original authors. Of course, those original books do not exist any more. But the good news is that many early copies were made, and some of these have survived through the centuries. (In fact, no other ancient book has so many existing early manuscript copies as the Bible has.) We can therefore have confidence that we do have, today, what was originally written down then. But those early manuscripts are written mainly in Hebrew and Greek – so, unless you are really fluent in those languages, they are not much good to you. Therefore, they have been translated into modern languages.

There are many different modern translations, all of which go back to the original text and seek to be as faithful as they can in conveying the meaning to us in a language that we can under-stand. But, of course, they do this slightly differently. Some concentrate on translating the words as accurately as possible – and produce a tight translation which may not read very fluently in English. Others concentrate on translating the meaning of each passage – and produce a loose paraphrase, which reads fluently but may not translate the words accurately. Still others strike a balance between the two – translating the words as accurately as possible, but producing something that can be read fairly easily.

One of these is the New International Version (NIV), which has become the most widely accepted translation around the world and has recently been updated as Today's New International Version (TNIV), with appropriate use of gender-inclusive language and modern idiom.

As a young Christian, you will probably find it very helpful to use the NIV or TNIV, plus one of the paraphrased editions, such as *The Message*.

Reading the Bible: Where do I start?

When I get a new book – whatever book it is, but particularly if it is a large one – I find it very helpful to dip into a few sections first, before I start reading from beginning to end. This helps me to get some overall idea of the content and makes it easier when I do read it all through. Of course, it is always helpful if someone who has already read the book suggests which bits I should dip into first – or, better still, gives me some kind of study guide. Let me see if I can help you in these ways with the Bible.

Scripture Union (www.scriptureunion.org.uk) and Bible Reading Fellowship (www.brf.org.uk) publish many study guides, in the form of daily Bible reading notes. Among their range you are bound to find one that will suit you. If you use these you will be able to read a part of the Bible each day and have an expert helping you to understand and apply it. Inter-Varsity Press publish several helpful resources, such as *The Bible with Pleasure* and *God's Big Picture*, which will help you get an overview of the Bible. *Discovering the New Testament* can help you get into the New Testament. The *New Bible Commentary* is an accessible guide to all the books of the Bible. However, nothing is as important as reading the Bible itself.

Useful as it is to read a short passage of the Bible every day, however, most of the books in the Bible were not designed to be read in that way. They were intended to be read through in their entirety – like any other book or letter. So how could you do this? First, three places to dip into:

1. Mark's Gospel. A short and very fast-paced account of the life and teaching of Jesus. I suggest that you read this through in one sitting.
2. John's Gospel. Having read Mark's account, now read John's. You will find this much more intimate and personal. If Mark's is like a television news report, then John's is more like a chat show.
3. Colossians. Now read a letter that was written to a group of young Christians who needed help to understand and grow in their new faith.

Having read these, and got some idea of the message of the Bible – the challenge now is to read the whole Bible all the way through, from Genesis to Revelation. As you do this, you might find the following brief outline helpful ...

Can you a give me a brief outline of the Bible?

There are many different ways of summarizing the content of the Bible. Here is one that I find particularly helpful.

Genesis 1 and 2 – God set it up
The first two chapters of the Bible tell us that God created this world and that he created men and women to live in it. He created us to live in a loving relationship with him, in a loving relationship with one another.

Genesis 3 – We mucked it up
Men and women chose to reject God, and we have all continued this by rejecting God in our own lives.

God came looking for Adam in the garden of Eden, but

couldn't find him – the relationship with God had been broken. Adam and Eve used fig-leaves to cover themselves, because there were things they wanted to hide from one another – the relationship with one another had been broken.

Genesis 4 to Malachi – God called us back
There are many things happening in the Old Testament and many different themes running through it. But, at its heart, it is the story of God calling men and women back to himself and to one another. God still loves us and wants us to come back into a proper relationship with himself and with other people.

Matthew to John – God came himself
Unfortunately, men and women keep rejecting God. So God came himself, in the person of his son, Jesus. He came to call us back into a proper relationship with himself and to provide a way for us to do that by dying for us on the cross. His death wasn't an accident – he intended to die and, in so doing, to take the death penalty that we deserve for everything wrong that we have ever done. We can now be forgiven; we can now come back into a proper relationship with God and with one another.

Acts to Jude – God grows relationships
God wants us to grow in our relationship with him and with one another; so he shows us how that can happen. On earth that relationship is growing, but still only partial. When we die, then we will enter into a perfect relationship with God and a perfect relationship with one another. The Bible calls it heaven.

Revelation – God is going to sort it out
God plans to restore the whole of creation to himself in a glorious victory over sin, death and evil at the end of time. Jesus will be the victorious king and will gather together all those who love him to share a wonderful eternity with him. There will be a brand new heaven and a brand new earth. But if we won't come back to God

and receive the forgiveness he offers, then the Bible is clear that our relationship with God and with other people will become increasingly broken. Ultimately we will face a total separation from God and from one another. The Bible calls it hell.

How can I understand the Bible better?

There are a number of different ways in which you can approach the Bible, each of which will help you to understand it better. Many years ago a student organization called The Navigators helped me to see the importance of five approaches: hearing it, reading it, studying it, memorizing it and meditating on it.

Hearing it read was the only way in which most Christians 'read' the Bible for most of the life of the church. It is only in recent years that most people have been able to read and to have their own copy of the Bible in their own language. So, if hearing the Bible being read helped Christians in the past, it will help you as well. You can do this by joining a small group where Christians read the Bible together – many church groups do this – or you could arrange one informally with two or three other Christian friends.

Reading the Bible for yourself gives you the opportunity to re-read passages – to go back over sections that you have not really understood. So you will find that you understand more by reading it yourself than by just hearing it read.

Studying the Bible enables you to understand even more – and, particularly, to benefit from the knowledge of others if you use a kind of handbook called a commentary. A commentary is a book all about one part of the Bible, written by an expert on it. It takes you through the Bible verse by verse, teaching you the back-ground to the passage; the meaning of the words; how this passage relates to other Bible passages; and so on. There are lots of different kinds of commentaries on sale in Christian bookshops. When studying the Bible in this way, it's also helpful to take notes.

Memorizing parts of the Bible is a wonderful approach to getting to know it better. Once you have learned a verse, you can repeat it over to yourself wherever you are. Often, through any day, you will have some spare time when it is not appropriate to get your Bible out – but if you have memorized verses, you can 'read' through them in your mind. You will also find that specific verses come back into your mind at particular times, especially when you are tempted. The Bible says 'I have hidden your word in my heart that I might not sin against you' (Psalm 119:11). I highly recommend learning certain key verses, especially, to get you started:

- Christ the centre
    2 Corinthians 5:17
    Galatians 2:20
- Obedience to Christ
    Romans 12:1
    John 14:21
- God's word
    2 Timothy 3:16
    Joshua 1:8
- Prayer
    John 15:7
    Philippians 4:6–7
- Fellowship
    Matthew 18:20
    Hebrews 10:24–25
- Witnessing
    Matthew 4:19
    Romans 1:16.

(taken from *The Topical Memory System*, NavPress)

Once you have memorized a verse, you will then find it easy to meditate on it. Christian meditation is not some irrational mystical process that is supposed to take you out of this world; rather it is a rational, practical process through which you get into the Bible and become more aware of God's presence with you in this world. To meditate literally means to 'consider deeply, reflect upon or revolve in the mind'. It is this 'revolving in the mind' that you will find particularly helpful as you meditate on Scripture. The process is fairly simple: just take a Bible passage and read it over and over again. Read it verse by verse, phrase by phrase and word by word. As you read it, put the emphasis on different verses, different phrases and different words and think about the meaning of each one. However, as you move deeper and deeper into the passage in this way, you must regularly take a step back out as well, to look at the context of the passage. Then you will be able to ensure that you are not taking the detail out of its proper context – within the other passages around it, the other books around it, and the whole Bible itself.

What do I do with what I learn from the Bible?

> Do not merely listen to the word and so deceive yourselves.
> Do what it says (James 1:22).

Imagine you are given a new Toyota car – the latest model. You would naturally be very excited. As with all cars, it comes with an owner's manual. Imagine treating that owner's manual like some Christians treat the Bible . . .

You read it and study it. You read a short passage every night and another every morning. You attend Toyota study groups, where you study it with other Toyota owners. You buy a coloured highlighter and mark the passages that are particularly helpful. You buy commentaries on it, and memorize it. You might even get really serious – and learn Japanese, so you can read it in the original!

Imagine that you did all these things – but never actually got in the car and drove it. What a waste! You would know everything about the car, but never experience it for yourself.

It is possible to treat the Bible like that. The Bible is very important; God will speak to us through it. But the Bible is not God; it simply leads us to God and enables us to hear him. The Bible is the signpost, not the destination; it is the love letter, not the lover.

So, as you read the Bible, don't just increase your knowledge – do what it says. The Bible is a practical manual, so look for practical ways in which you can respond to what it says. Here are some practical questions you can ask yourself as you read it:

- Is there a promise to believe?
- Is there an example to follow?
- Is there a command to obey?
- Is there an error to avoid?

God will speak to us through the Bible, but this is not primarily to give us information; rather, it is to change and guide our lives.

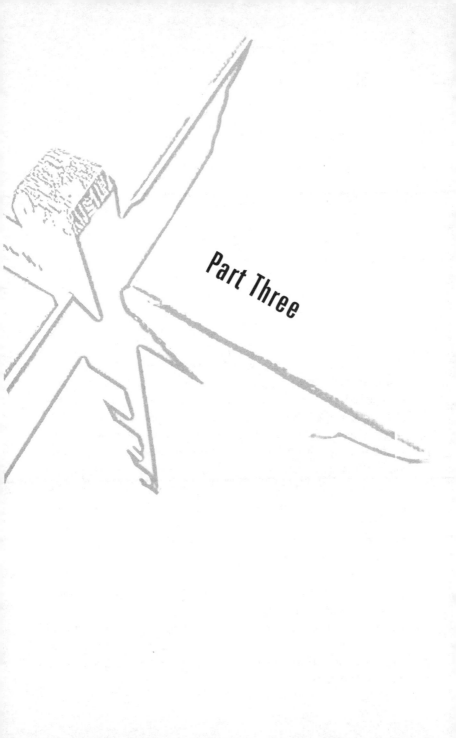

Part Three

11

What do I do first?

Nick Pollard

If you're not quite sure whether you have really become a Christian, then this chapter is for you. Over the years many people have asked me 'How do I become a Christian?' My response has always been the same – to point them to the place in the Bible where other people asked very much the same question.

If you have not yet become a Christian, but want to, then let's look at that same place – which you will find in the book called 'Acts'. This tells the story of the early church and how they led people to faith in Jesus. In the second chapter we find Peter preaching to thousands of people in Jerusalem. The Bible then records, 'When the people heard this, they were cut to the heart and said to Peter and the other apostles, "Brothers, what shall we do?"' (Acts 2:37).

That is really the same question that you might be asking: 'How do I become a Christian?' Peter gives them the answer. And then he says 'The promise is for you and your children and for all who are far off' (Acts 2:39). That means that this answer is as relevant to you today as it was to the people in Jerusalem two thousand years ago.

And what is the answer? 'Repent and be baptized, every one of you, in the name of Jesus Christ for the forgiveness of your sins. And you will receive the gift of the Holy Spirit' (Acts 2:38).

If you look at this, you will see that there are two things to do and two things to receive. We are to repent and to be baptized; we are to receive the forgiveness of our sins and the gift of the Holy Spirit. Let's look at these in some more detail.

First, we are to repent. That word means literally to 'change your mind'. So there is change that must take place – and that change happens to your mind.

If you are serious about becoming a Christian, you will be willing to change. You will want to follow Jesus and you know that you weren't doing that before. You will want to do the things that God wants you to do and you will be willing for any changes that have to take place.

It is rather like any relationship – all relationships mean change; you don't stay the same. So how much more will coming into a relationship with the holy God mean change. The question is whether you are willing to accept whatever changes God needs to bring about in your life. Because, if you are not, then you are not ready to become a Christian. You cannot come to faith in Christ and carry on the same way as before – you couldn't do that with any real relationship.

Let me give you an illustration. When I was young I was a natural practical joker. I just couldn't resist practical jokes. I was the one who would tie your shoe laces together – so when you stood up you would fall over. If you took me on a church weekend away – I was the one who put cling-film over the toilet.

But when I started going out with Carol (who later became my wife), I discovered that she hated practical jokes. I realized that, particularly, one night when we were out for a motorcycle ride. I used to have a big Triumph motorbike (I used to say it was a triumph if I managed to get the thing started), and we were out on it when I had to stop for petrol. We both got off the bike and I filled it up. Then I got on, started it up (eventually) and called

Carol to get on behind me. Just as she was swinging her leg across, I had a brilliant idea. I thought it would be really funny. And I timed it exactly right – as she got on I pulled away and she went down flat. Looking back on it now, I do realize that you have to have a pretty well-developed sense of humour to see the funny side of sitting in a pool of oil on a cold garage forecourt. And I realized that night that Carol does not like practical jokes – because she came over and hit me.

So I had a choice to make. Either I could say, 'This is the way that I am – I am not willing to change,' – and I would have to recognize that my relationship with Carol would go nowhere – or I could say, 'I love Carol so much, and I so much want to be with her, that I am willing to change.'

Are you willing to change in whatever way you need to – so you can follow Jesus?

Perhaps you are not sure, because you are wondering what you need to change. Well, the word 'repentance' tells you the answer. It means, literally, 'change your mind' – so it is your mind that has to change.

At this stage it is not your behaviour which has to change. That is, you don't have to achieve a certain standard of behaviour in order to become a Christian. A relationship with God is not a reward for good behaviour. Once you have become a Christian, you will find that your behaviour does change – but that will happen gradually. All that is required at the moment is that you change your mind, so that you don't want to do what is wrong and you are willing to do what is right; you want to stop disobeying God and you are willing to obey him; you want to stop going your own way and you are willing to follow Jesus – wherever he takes you, and whatever it costs.

Similarly, it is not your emotions that have to change. Although, once your mind has changed, your emotions will gradually follow, God does not require you to have a certain type of feelings in order to come to know him. All he asks is that you change your mind, so you are willing to feel the same way that he does.

How can you know if you really are ready to repent? Perhaps one way is to think of one thing that you are doing that you know is wrong. There will be one thing that comes to your mind. You know that this thing is not right. You know this is not how God wants you to be. So now the question is – if you really want to repent – are you willing to change in at least that one area? I am not asking whether you think you can change your behaviour. (No doubt you won't be able to on your own. That is why you need to come into a relationship with God: so he can give you the power to change.) Nor am I asking if you feel differently about that wrong thing. (No doubt you will still feel an emotional attachment to it – that is why you need God to change your feelings.) All I am asking is whether you are prepared to change your mind about it – whether you are willing to let go of that wrong thing, whatever it costs.

And cost is important. There is a sense in which becoming a Christian costs you nothing – and a sense in which it costs you everything. As we will discover below, it costs you nothing in the sense that there is nothing you can do to earn your relationship with God. There is no price you can pay. Jesus has already paid that price on your behalf. But there is a sense in which it costs you everything – because you are changing your mind and saying that you are willing to follow Jesus in any way he calls you.

You will have noticed that I keep using the word 'willing' instead of 'wanting'. That is because repentance is an act of your will, as you say 'I will follow Jesus', and because it requires you to be willing for any changes – even ones that you may not actually want.

Let me give you an illustration. If you decided you wanted to become a great Olympic athlete you would probably need to make changes in your life. You would need a disciplined and rigorous training schedule. You would have to get fit and go out in all kinds of weather, and you would need to control your diet, forgoing big puddings and all the things that would not help your running. You might still want to eat those things, but you would be willing to say no.

Are you willing to say no to the things that you know are wrong in your life? Are you willing to follow Jesus whatever it costs? If so, you are repenting.

The Bible then tells us to be baptized. Does this mean that we have to nip down to the local river in order to become a Christian? Not necessarily. Although baptism is clearly important, and if you haven't been baptized you will need to get baptized as soon as possible, what matters at this stage is that you understand the fact that baptism was a public sign. It was something that was done in full view of other people. It was a way of telling everyone that this person was now following Jesus. Are you ready for that?

Many people tell me that their faith is personal and private. Well, the Bible says that they are half right. Our faith must be personal, but not private. Baptism was not a private affair carried out in a little church with the doors closed. It was a very public event carried out in an open river. If I asked you now, would you be prepared to go down to the river and be baptized publicly, with all your friends and family present? Are you willing to tell people that you have now become a Christian, and that from now on you want to follow Jesus?

This public acknowledgment of your new faith is very important. First, it shows that you really are serious about following Jesus; second, it enables you to establish the relationship you have with other Christians now that you too are part of the church; and third, it signals to everybody that you are now a follower of Jesus.

If you are ready to repent and to publicly acknowledge that you are following Jesus – then we can move on to the two things which God has promised you.

First, he promises that you will receive forgiveness of your sins. It is important that you understand why this is.

He is offering to forgive you because he loves you. God has an unconditional love for you. He doesn't love you because you are beautiful (perhaps you are). He doesn't love you because you are good (possibly you may be). He loves you because he loves you – because he loves you. There is nothing that you can do that will make God love you more – or make him love you less. So there is nothing you can do to earn his love.

Then, he is able to forgive you because Jesus died on the cross for you. When Jesus died he took the penalty that you deserve for everything wrong you have ever done and are ever going to do in the future. Those wrong things lead to separation from God, and to death. But Jesus has taken those consequences for us.

Sin separates you from God – in very much the same way that sin separates any relationship. Suppose you have a friend and you lie to them, or cheat them. You have sinned against them. The result is that the friendship will be spoilt; there will be an awkwardness, a barrier, between you. As we sin against God, we put up a barrier between us and him.

Sin also leads to death. It kills our relationships; it kills our value; it kills spiritual life; and, ultimately, it kills our very souls. Even if someone doesn't acknowledge that they are sinning, the very process of ignoring the sin actually leads to death in that person. Initially, when that person sins, they will be aware that they have done something wrong; their conscience will cry out to them. But if they ignore it, and stifle their conscience, then the next time they sin their conscience will be weaker – and the next time it will be weaker still. So, as a person sins, they are killing off a part of themselves.

Now, when Jesus died on the cross, he was taking your death onto himself. He died in your place, so that you might have your life back. And when, in death, he was separated from God – he took your separation onto himself. He was separated in your place, so that you might be restored into a relationship with God.

That is why you can be forgiven – because the price has been paid. God is not 'letting you off' for your sin. He is not saying 'Sin doesn't really matter; let's forget about it.' The fact is that sin does really matter. There are consequences; there is a price to pay. But God is offering to take that price on himself, in your place.

Let me give you an illustration. Imagine I have been driving too fast in my car. I am caught by the police and I am brought before the court. I know that I am guilty, so I prepare to plead 'guilty'. Then the judge comes in, and I recognize who he is – he is my favourite uncle. I think to myself, 'I'm all right now – he is my uncle. He loves me; he cares for me; he wants the best for me.' But my uncle says, 'You have pleaded guilty to this offence – I cannot just let you off. If I did, then I would be saying that your offence did not matter – and it does. So I have to fine you the proper fine of £100.' My jaw drops. 'But, uncle,' I say to him, 'I thought you loved me; I thought you cared about me. You have stood up for justice – but where is your love?' Just then my uncle gets up from the bench, comes over to me, and writes out a cheque for £100, saying, 'But I will pay the fine for you – will you take my cheque?'

There is a sense in which God is offering you a cheque to pay for all of your sin – past, present and future. When Jesus hung on that cross he showed that sin matters – everything you have ever done matters. It can't be just ignored; you can't be simply let off. If he did that, then nothing would ever really matter; there would be no right or wrong; everyone could do what they wanted; and everything would be ruined. But he also showed that he loves you and he wants to take the consequence of your sin – off your shoulders and onto his.

This doesn't mean that we would take sin lightly; quite the opposite. We will take it even more seriously, because we realize what it cost God to provide our forgiveness for us. In a sense, every time we sin we are loading another sin on Jesus' back. Each time we sin we are banging a nail in a little harder; we are pushing the spear in a little further.

But it does mean that you can know that you are forgiven, because it doesn't depend on you and what you do – it relies upon God and what he did in sending Jesus to die for you.

Now, second, he promises to give you the gift of his Holy Spirit. Again, it is important that you understand what this means.

Becoming a Christian is a supernatural event. It is not simply accepting some new philosophy, nor ticking off a list of beliefs, nor adopting a code to live by. Rather, it is coming into such an intimate relationship with God that he even comes to live inside you, by his Holy Spirit.

Let me explain what this means – and what it doesn't mean.

First, what it means. God has revealed himself to us as a Trinity: that means three persons in one. He is God the Father – who is above us; God the Son – who came to be with us and to die for us; and God the Holy Spirit – who comes to live inside us.

Jesus described it in this way:

> I will ask the Father, and he will give you another advocate to help you and be with you for ever – the Spirit of truth ... you know him, for he lives with you and will be in you. I will not leave you as orphans; I will come to you ... you will realize that I am in my Father, and you are in me, and I am in you (John 14:16–20).

Here Jesus talks of the Trinity. He himself, the Son, says he will ask the Father, who will send the Holy Spirit. But see how he describes this Holy Spirit. He says, 'he lives with you', and he says, 'I will come to you'. This is one of the great mysteries of God, that theologians have struggled to understand for centuries: God is one God but in three persons. The Holy Spirit is not some separate God; he is the God who created us, and who came to us in the person of Jesus. But, whereas God the Father is in heaven, and God the Son has returned to sit at his right hand, God the Holy Spirit comes to live inside us. (You can read some more about the Trinity in chapter 9.)

So when you become a Christian, you are asking God to come and live inside you. You are asking him to be right there in the centre of your life: not just someone that you go to every now and then in your prayers, but someone who is actually in the driving seat, leading and guiding you. He will always be with you, giving you the power to live God's way in God's world.

Living with God in the centre of your life is a great adventure – as he leads you and guides you along difficult paths, but gives you the power to overcome the obstacles and temptations along the way. It is interesting to compare characters in the Bible who had received God's Holy Spirit with those who hadn't. In the Old Testament we see many great people who sought to follow God, but who fell into sin in some disastrous way. However, in the New Testament we see great people whose lives were not damaged in this way. What is the difference? In the New Testament they had received God's Holy Spirit. And so will you, when you become a Christian. This doesn't mean that you won't sin, but it does mean that you won't have to.

Now, let's see what receiving God's Holy Spirit doesn't mean. When Peter said 'you will receive the gift of the Holy Spirit' he didn't say 'you will receive a warm fuzzy feeling'. In fact the Bible doesn't really say anything about feelings at all.

When some people become Christians they experience a particularly strong, sometimes overwhelming, feeling. Others don't. It's just like getting married. When I was a boy I sang in the parish church choir, and I must have seen hundreds of weddings. I noticed that some people, when they got married, clearly experienced a tremendous feeling. Some laughed; some cheered; some even fainted. But most people didn't appear to feel anything special. However, they all could not have been in any doubt that, through the vows they had declared and the promises they had received, they were indeed married. In the same way, different people have different experiences when they enter into a relationship with God through Jesus. But whatever you feel or don't feel, if you truly repent and are willing to declare publicly that you are now following Jesus, and you ask God to forgive you and to come and live inside you by his Holy Spirit – then you can be sure that he will do that.

So, now, the question is: are you ready to do this?

I never want to push anyone into anything. But I expect that, if you have read this far, you will know whether you are prepared to take this crucial step of becoming a Christian.

Let me tell you how I can help you to do this. Below I am going to write out a prayer. It is a prayer that enables you to declare to God that you repent of your sins, that you want to receive his forgiveness, that you want to follow Jesus and that you invite him to come and live inside you by his Holy Spirit.

I suggest that you read it through for yourself first – to ensure that you can pray it and really mean it. Then, if you are sure that you are ready to do this, I suggest you pray it out loud, slowly, sentence by sentence – thinking about each line as you say it. If it is possible, you might find it helpful to go to a Christian friend right now and tell them that you want to pray this prayer in front of them, with their support and help. But you don't have to. Ultimately, the prayer is between you and God. He is there with you. He will hear you. He will respond to you.

So here is the prayer:

Lord God, I am sorry for all my sins;
Please forgive me.
Thank you that Jesus died for me – so I can be forgiven.
Right now, I give my whole life to you.
From now on I want to serve you and follow you – whatever the
    cost.
Please come and live inside me;
Please make me clean;
Please enable me to live for you.
In Jesus' name,
Amen.

If you have prayed that and meant it, then you can be sure that God has heard and has answered. You have come into a new relationship with God – like being born again, as Jesus calls it – and new people need help. No doubt you will be wondering: what do I do now? That is why we wrote this book – so I suggest you turn to the beginning and see how you can, now, go on and grow in your new-found faith.